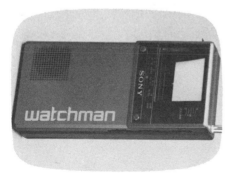

Television and Society

An Investigative Approach

Charles S. Ungerleider
Associate Professor
Department of Social and
Educational Studies
Faculty of Education
University of British Columbia
Vancouver, British Columbia

Ernest Krieger
Co-ordinator
Social Studies Department
Sentinel Secondary School
West Vancouver, British Columbia

Irwin Publishing
Toronto   Canada

Canadian Cataloguing in Publication Data

Ungerleider, Charles S.
  Television and society

Includes index.
ISBN 0-7725-1518-2

1. Television broadcasting — Social aspects —
Canada.   2. Television broadcasting — Canada —
History.   I. Krieger, Ernest, 1949- .   II. Title.

PN1992.6.U53 1985   384.55'4'0971   C85-098116-6

Text and cover design: Robert Garbutt Productions
Cover photos: *(crowd)* Photo Centre/NFB Photothèque,
  ONF (photo by Bryce Flynn); PAC/NFTSA — CBC Collection
Typeset by Q Composition Incorporated
Printed in Canada by T.H. Best Printing Company Ltd.

    3 4 5 6 THB 90 89 88 87

Published by Irwin Publishing Inc.
180 West Beaver Creek Road
Richmond Hill, Ontario L4B 1B4

Acknowledgements

The authors and publisher wish to thank the following individuals and organizations for permission to include the illustrations listed. Every effort has been made to acknowledge correctly the sources of the illustrations. The publisher welcomes any information that will enable him to rectify, in subsequent printings, any errors or omissions which may have been made in crediting the photographs.

6, 7, 9, & 11 / Historical Pictures Service, Inc., Chicago.   18 & 20 / Miller Services Ltd. (American Stock Photo; H. Armstrong Roberts Photo).
21 / PAC/NFTSA – CBC Collection.   22 / Miller Services Ltd. (H. Armstrong Roberts Photo).
25 / CBC Photo (Robert C. Ragsdale Limited Photo).
28 / The Archives, Eaton's of Canada Limited.
33, 36, 37, 40 & 41 / PAC/NFTSA – CBC Collection.
43 / Sony of Canada Ltd. 47 / Canapress Photo Service (AP Photo).   48 / PAC/NFTSA – CBC Photo.
51 / Miller Services Ltd. (Harold M. Lambert Photo).
66, 67, 68, 70, 74, & 76 / CBC Photo (Fred Phipps Photos; dancer in studio, Gilbert Milne Photo).
79 / PAC/NFTSA – CBC Collection.   86 / From Camera script of the 5th Draft of Episode #15, "Operation Grandad," *Hangin' In*, CBC Production, courtesy Carol Commisso, Associate Producer.
88 / (top) Miller Services Ltd. (H. Armstrong Roberts Photo); (bottom) PAC/NFTSA – CBC Collection. 89 / CBC Photo (Fred Phipps).   90 & 91 / Courtesy David Barlow.   94 / From Camera script of the 5th Draft of Episode #15, "Operation Grandad", *Hangin' In*, CBC Production, courtesy Carol Commisso, Associate Producer.   94, 97, & 101 / CBC Photo (Robert C. Ragsdale Photo, 2 Fred Phipps Photos).   109 / PAC/NFTSA – CBC Collection.
111 / CBC Photo (Fred Phipps Photo).   113 / CTV Television Network Ltd.   116 / CBC Photo.
117 & 121 / Canapress Photo Service (CP Photo).
124 / Historical Pictures Sercice, Inc., Chicago.
128 / CTV Television Network Ltd.   129 / PAC/NFTSA—CBC Collection.   138 / Canapress Photo Service (AP Photo).   140 / PAC/NFTSA – CBC Collection.   146 / CTV Television Network Ltd.   149 & 153 / Canapress Photo Service (CP Photos).   160 & 161 / The Archives, Eaton's of Canada Limited.   167 / PAC/NFTSA – CBC Collection.   172 / Canapress Photo Service (Wide World Photo).   175 / PAC/NFTSA – Crawley Films Collection.   190 / Suzanne Firth.   194 / Ontario Ministry of Industry and Tourism.   206 / PAC/NFTSA – CBC Collection.   209 / CBC Photo (Fred Phipps).   211 / Canapress Photo Service.
216 / CTV Television Network Ltd.   217 / Sony of Canada Ltd.

Irwin Publishing Inc. acknowledges the financial support of the Government of Canada through the Canadian Studies Directorate of the Department of the Secretary of State of Canada.

*To Mary, Helena,
Jessica, Suzanne,
Nina, and Sasha*

*(with apologies to
Percy Saltzman
and Pinky Lee)*

Contents

Tuning In To Television

"To study television is to study the way people live their lives."

A Challenge To Students

Television and Society was written for curious students who like to examine things for themselves. This is the reason we have used the subtitle "an investigative approach." According to our dictionary, *investigate* means "to examine carefully to learn the facts about something hidden, unique or complex."

Throughout the book you will find investigations. The investigations focus on questions about television and its impact on Canadian society. They have been designed to stimulate your curiosity and to provide an opportunity for you to become actively involved in the study of television. We have indicated by a set of numbers at the end of each investigation the skills you are developing when you carry out that particular investigation. The explanation for the numbers is given in Appendix I at the back of the book, "Skills Developed by Doing the Investigations."

In a few investigations we suggest that you videotape material from television programs and commercials. Copyright laws require that you obtain permission, in writing, from the appropriate television station before you record the material you need. When writing for permission, be sure to state why you want to videotape the material and that its use will be confined to the classroom.

Language is a major vehicle for the transmission of culture. It is misleading to assume that observations about the impact of television on one linguistic group will apply to the members of other groups. The focus of this book is on the impact of television on English-speaking Canadians. An examination of the impact of

Recognition of the importance of the television medium in the educational system and a spread of that awareness throughout the population should be, in my view, one of the top priorities on the nation's agenda.

MARTIN ESSLIN, *The Age of Television*

television on French-speaking Canadians merits study in its own right.

By the time you have completed *Television and Society* you will be able to answer many questions about television and its impact on English-speaking Canadians. For example, you will be able to suggest how television has affected and continues to affect the distribution of political power within Canada. You will begin to form opinions about how television influences people's perceptions of political issues, the selection of their political leaders, and their feelings of powerfulness and powerlessness.

The text and the investigations will help you form a point of view about how television affects how people see themselves as consumers, their definition of the "good life," their concept of prestige, and their feelings of what makes economic success. You will also develop an appreciation of how the relations among members of different cultural, ethnic and social groups within society have changed as a result of television.

You will learn how television affects the ideas people hold and the way ideas are transmitted from one person to another. You will be able to show how people's values have changed as a result of television. You will be able to suggest answers to such questions as: Does television shape or reflect a society's values? To what extent does television allow for the expression of ideas that run counter to society's dominant ideas?

Tips for Getting the Most from this Book

There are a number of ways you can increase your understanding of the ideas and information contained in this book. Read carefully and take notes. Developing a useful set of notes is mostly a matter of organization.

Television and Society is organized into chapters. Within chap-

> I can preach to more people in one night on TV than perhaps Paul did in his whole lifetime.
>
> BILLY GRAHAM, American evangelist

ters, the material is organized by using subsections. The material is divided within subsections by paragraphs which are organized around a main idea. Construct a topic outline using these sub-divisions. The outline will help you to understand and remember what you have read.

You can also increase your understanding of the ideas in the book by testing yourself. Most of the chapters in *Television and Society* include questions you can use to test your grasp of the main ideas in the chapter. The most difficult questions are those which ask you to evaluate ideas. The answers to these questions cannot be found on one or two pages of the book. You must discuss these questions with one another and with your teacher to develop the most meaningful answers.

Another way of increasing understanding is to keep a journal of your thoughts and reactions. Make entries in the journal on a regular basis. Plan to write a minimum of one paragraph for each class session and each reading assignment.

The following questions may help you to get started: Did the class session or reading assignment raise a question or issue of importance that you would like to pursue further? Did the pres-entation of the material overlook some idea that needs explo-ration? Did the point of view being expressed consider the assumptions or evidence carefully? Were there assumptions that were not fully examined or evidence that was ignored? Do not hesitate to go beyond these "starter" questions in pursuing the idea or ideas of importance to you.

Another way to increase understanding is to carry out the investigations presented in each chapter. The investigations have been designed to provide you with direct experience with an issue or topic addressed in the book. They are designed to be carried out by groups of students working together.

You can also increase your understanding of the material in

■ **Investigation 1.1:** *To Understand How Television Has Changed Canadian Society*

Method: ***Most Canadians under 35 years of age do not realize what life was like before television was introduced into Canadian society.***

1. Using a tape recorder, interview a person who grew up without television. Have the person describe his or her childhood.

2. Select several interviews for presentation to the class.

3. Discuss the differences between your life and the lives of the people you interviewed. How many of the differences can be connected to the presence or absence of television?

4. Write a short essay entitled: *Why I would, or would not, like to have lived before the age of television.*

Skills Developed: **3.1; 3.5; 4.1; 4.2; 4.4**

Television and Society by making good use of the Glossary at the end of the book. The first time a word or phrase that is defined in the Glossary appears in the text it is printed in boldface type.

Putting Television Into Focus

Every textbook needs a set of ideas to put the material being studied into focus. The process is much like viewers adjusting the fine tuning on their television sets. Viewers can probably enjoy television simply by accepting the picture the way they find it when the picture first appears. However, if the picture is a bit fuzzy, they can greatly increase their enjoyment by adjusting the fine tuning.

One way to put things into focus is to develop a set of ideas in relation to one topic and, then, apply the same ideas to another topic. The material that follows develops a set of ideas about the influence of the development of printing on people's lives. You should then be able to relate these ideas to the impact that *television* has had on people's lives.

The Invention of Printing

Those of you who are reading this book enjoy a skill that even today is denied to almost 800 million people in the world, including many Canadians. Reading is such a common occurrence in some people's lives that they take it for granted. But, for many people in the world, the fact that they cannot read keeps them powerless.

People who can read have much more control over their lives than people who cannot. Imagine what your world would be like if you could not read. It would be difficult to find out the time and place of Friday night's movie or concert. The standings of a hockey or baseball team would not be easy to find. How would you follow the street signs to your favourite restaurant? And once there, how would you order from the menu?

Without the ability to read, people looking for jobs cannot use the classified advertisements in the newspaper. Even if they did find someone offering a job, their lack of ability to read would probably still prevent them from getting the job, since they wouldn't be able to fill in the application form.

The ability to understand the printed word is so important in our society that a large part of the time spent in school is devoted to learning about print. Most students spend the bulk of their time learning how to read and how to understand what they are reading.

Magazines, comic books, newspapers, novels, textbooks, and

A fifteenth-century monk hard at work copying books by hand. Before the invention of printing from moveable type, costly, handwritten manuscripts were read only by a wealthy, literate elite.

posters announcing the latest dance or rock concert — almost everywhere we turn we are surrounded by printed material produced by high-speed machinery. Printed material is so common and plentiful that it is hard to imagine what our lives would be like without it.

Historians claim that the invention of printing — or more precisely, the invention of moveable type and the printing press — brought about changes in almost every area of society. They suggest that these changes were so great that society after the invention of printing was as different from society before the invention of printing as night is different from day.

Before the invention of moveable type and the printing press all books were written out and copied by hand. Some people spent their entire working lives slowly copying books with quills and reeds. In the early 1400s, Europeans began to use block printing in which characters and pictures were carved onto blocks of wood. "Block books" were produced by binding block prints together. Both hand copying and block printing were extremely slow processes, with the result that very few books were produced in a year. The development of moveable type and the printing press dramatically changed the speed at which books could be reproduced. The first printing press printed 300 sheets a day.

The first printed materials from printing presses using moveable type were a Bible and some Church documents produced in 1454. Within a dozen years, printing presses were operating regularly in Rome. By the early sixteenth century, book publishers could be found in every large European city. And, by the end of the century there was an established international book trade. From that time until the development of sound and picture reproduction processes (radio, telephone, motion pictures, and television), the printed word was the main way that ideas and information were spread.

In the mid-1400s Johannes Gutenberg invented the type mould. The uniform metal letters made printing from moveable type practical for the first time. This is a page from Gutenberg's Bible, the first book printed using the new technology.

Seventeenth-century German printing and publishing house. Gutenberg's invention of the type mould made it possible to have a sufficient supply of uniform metal letters to set a book into type. Once the type was in place, large numbers of books could be printed.

The invention of moveable type and the printing press helped to spread literacy — the ability to read and write. Before the invention, very few people knew how to read and write. Those who did exercised considerable power and influence. As larger numbers of people began to read and write, the power of the few people who previously had held a monopoly on literacy was greatly reduced.

As more and more people learned to read and write they began to examine and often to criticize the ideas and actions of the Church and the government. In reaction, governments and the Church drew up laws censoring what could be printed, in an attempt to maintain control over what people thought and believed. These attempts to control information and ideas only slowed the changes printing brought about. Hidden presses made

it possible for people to produce written materials criticizing the activities of the political and religious leaders of the day.

The invention of printing also changed language, literature and art. The development of the printing press made it possible for people to have careers as authors. Books rather than speech became the standard for the correct use of language. Local speech differences began to give way to the language used in the centres of learning and trade. English-speaking peoples began to write the language of London. French-speaking peoples began to write the language of Paris. In other words, the invention of printing made it possible to focus attention on uniform grammatical standards in a way that hadn't been possible when language was entirely spoken.

The invention of printing influenced the creation of libraries and other places where information could be assembled, stored and distributed in large quantities. Reference books such as dictionaries, almanacs and encyclopaediae made knowledge available. Before the invention of printing, such information could not have been gathered together in an entire lifetime of work.

Before the spread of literacy and the widespread distribution of printed material, very few people actually saw famous works of art. Those few who did read or who had access to the original works were used to seeing them in colour. By the time printed material was being widely distributed, many people were able to see famous artwork. But the printed copies of artwork were mostly reproduced in black and white.

Until books were available to many people, the most common way to use a book was for one person to read it aloud to others. After mass printing, people more commonly read to themselves. This led to a related change. Books that had been produced to be "heard" became less common as books were produced to be "read". This change in emphasis meant, for example, that the amount of poetry produced, much of which had been written to

The invention of the printing
press led to the establishment of
the first libraries.

be listened to, declined. At the same time the amount of prose
produced, written to be read not listened to, dramatically increased.

After printing was invented, the ability to memorize ideas and
information became a less valuable skill. Passing on traditions
from one generation to the next by word of mouth also became
less vital and historical accounts became more accurate. Printing
made it possible for people to communicate their ideas to people
they would never see or know.

For centuries the supremacy of print went unchallenged. But,
as further developments in technology occurred, print was forced
to share its position of importance with other media of mass
communication, bringing further social changes.

Making Orderly Observations

People use a variety of techniques for organizing their thinking about complicated events such as the impact of printing or television on society. One technique is to group items which seem closely related. Using this technique, the changes described in the material you have just read can be grouped under five headings: technological changes, political changes, economic changes, social changes, and intellectual changes.

A *technological change* is any change in the way people provide themselves with the material objects they use. Such changes may include anything from the development of a new method of opening canned goods to the development of a spaceship for travelling outside the earth's atmosphere.

In "The Invention of Printing," one major technological change was discussed: the *change from hand lettering manuscripts to printing manuscripts with moveable type on a printing press*. Once the type had been set many copies of a book could be easily and quickly produced.

"The Invention of Printing" also outlined a number of *political changes* that occurred as a result of the development of printing. Political change is any change that alters the way power is distributed among people. In any group, the way that power is distributed can range from all members sharing authority equally to a situation in which one member has and uses all of the power.

Two political changes were mentioned. *The powers of government and the Church were reduced.* This happened because as more people learned to read and write as a result of the greater availability of printed material, they became more knowledgeable about and more critical of Church and government. With the increased number of printing presses, people were able to produce and distribute material criticizing the way the Church and government handled their affairs.

William Caxton's *The Game and Play of Chess* was the first book printed in English with moveable type.

The second and related political change was the *establishment of censorship laws*. This was one way governments and the Church reacted to the criticisms that people had begun to make.

Economic changes affect the distribution of goods and services. Three such changes were mentioned: *the establishment of careers as authors, the establishment of book publishing as a commercial enterprise*, and *the establishment of an international trade in books*.

The technological, political and economic changes were accompanied by social and intellectual changes. *Social changes* affect the relationships among groups in a society. *Intellectual changes* are changes in people's ideas.

Of the changes mentioned, the following can be roughly classified as social because they eventually affected how people related to one another. The fact that *more people could read and write* changed the relations between those who were and those who were not informed about the society in which they lived.

People could now read by themselves. Before the invention of moveable type and the spread of literacy, people had to rely on others to learn what was contained in printed material. Being able to read for one's self was a major step in making people less dependent upon the few literate members of the group.

People could put their ideas in writing. *Written material made people less dependent upon word of mouth as a way of communicating their traditions to the next generation*. It also made them *less dependent on their memories for record keeping* and helped to make historical accounts more reliable.

Once printed material and literacy were spread throughout society, *people could more easily communicate with others*. Passing on information from one generation to another or transmitting information across vast physical distances became easier with the spread of literacy and the printing press.

In "The Invention of Printing" we talked about five intellectual changes: *people were in a better position to question the ideas of the Church and the government; copies of famous artworks were widely distributed; the proportion of prose material in relation to poetry increased; libraries and reference works were established; and grammatical forms were standardized.*

"The Invention of Printing" demonstrates two principles that have been observed over the years. The first is: *In every society, five systems* — technological, political, economic, social, and intellectual — *are interconnected.*

Figure 1.1: *The Connections Among Society's Systems*

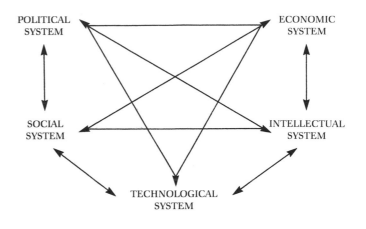

The second principle is: *Changes in one system of activity influence changes in the other systems.* For example, the technological change of the invention of moveable type and the printing press led to changes in all other areas of society.

■ **Investigation 1.2:**   *To Understand How Television Influences The Lives Of Canadians And The Communities In Which They Live*

Method: **The development of television has been compared to the invention of moveable type and the printing press as one of the most significant inventions in history. It is, of course, difficult to isolate television's influence from that of other aspects of modern life. One way to evaluate television's impact is to consider what life would be like without television.**

1. Make a list of all the changes you believe would occur in Canadian life if television was eliminated. You should consider the changes that would take place in education, the economy, family life, recreation, politics, etc.

2. After you have made your list, divide your entries into positive and negative results.

3. In class, discuss or debate the question: *Is television a positive presence in Canadian society?*

Skills Developed: 1.21; 1.25; 2.1; 3.4; 3.5

Test Yourself

A. *Identification:*   Explain the meaning and/or significance of the following in your own words.

moveable type	literacy
censorship	technology
technological change	economic change
social change	political change
intellectual change	interconnected

B. *Multiple Choice:* For each question, indicate which response you think best answers the question.

1. Before the invention of moveable type and the printing press:
   a. it didn't matter whether people could read or write.
   b. literate and illiterate people had equal power.
   c. we have no evidence about how power was distributed in society.
   d. the literate minority held most of the power.

2. Before the invention of moveable type and the printing press:
   a. people in the same country spoke and wrote in different ways.
   b. people in the same country spoke and wrote in the same way.
   c. memory was less important than it is today.
   d. people were more likely to challenge existing authority than they are today.

3. The establishment of censorship laws as a result of the invention of printing is an example of:
   a. social change.
   b. political change.
   c. economic change.
   d. intellectual change.

4. In observing that the invention of printing caused a reduction in the influence of the literate elite, one can state that:
   a. social change may cause intellectual change.
   b. economic change may cause technological change.
   c. technological change may cause political change.
   d. technological change may cause social change.

5. Which of the following factors related to the invention of printing would most accurately explain the increase in literacy?
   a. the expansion of public education

    b. the increase in the amount of knowledge

    c. the development of public libraries

    d. the decrease in the cost of books due to mechanical production

6. With the invention of printing, poetry declined in favour of prose because:

    a. books were read silently by individuals instead of aloud to crowds.

    b. with the declining importance of memory people could not memorize poems.

    c. poetry was never popular with many people both before or after the invention of printing.

    d. authors could make a better living writing prose than by writing poetry.

7. Whose power was most sharply reduced due to the invention of printing?

    a. business people

    b. kings

    c. the Church

    d. peasants

8. How many of the world's 4.5 billion people are illiterate today?

    a. 100 million

    b. 400 million

    c. 800 million

    d. 1.2 billion

9. The printing press was invented in the:

    a. tenth century

    b. thirteenth century

    c. fifteenth century

    d. nineteenth century

10. Which of the following was NOT the result of the invention of printing?
   a. The importance of memory declined.
   b. The first universities were opened.
   c. The cost of books decreased.
   d. The distribution of power in society changed.

C. *Activities for Further Investigation*

1. In this chapter you read about five kinds of change: technological, political, economic, social, and intellectual. All five forces are present in any society. Scholars often argue about which of these forces for change is most important. Some suggest that economic forces are the most important and that all other kinds of change flow from economic changes. Others believe that changes in ideas (intellectual change) cause most of the changes in other areas.

In a brief essay, consider whether any one kind of change is the most important as the source of all other kinds of change. Support your ideas with reference to specific examples of change.

2. Prior to the introduction of television, radio was the chief entertainment medium for most Canadians. In addition to music and news, radio featured dramatic programs, mysteries, comedies, sporting events and quiz programs. With the advent of television, radio lost much of its audience. Radio was forced to change its content and format in order to survive.

In an essay, evaluate the roles of television and radio in your life. Do television and radio compete for your attention or does each meet different entertainment and educational needs? What aspects of each medium do you find most and least attractive?

3. In an essay, comment on the following statement: "Progress in society is not the result of the increase of human intelligence, but of the increased ability of people to store and transmit information."

4. In the section about the invention of printing, it was stated that "until the development of sound and picture reproduction processes (radio, telephone, motion pictures, and television), the printed word was the main way that ideas and information were spread." Many people today believe that the replacement of the printed word by electronic media (television, computers, etc.) has been a step backwards. In an essay, indicate whether you are concerned about the declining importance of the printed word in today's society.

5. The printing press is just one of many inventions that have had a profound impact on society. One historian has suggested, for example, that the invention of the stirrup and trousers were major factors contributing to the fall of the Roman Empire. What invention do you believe has caused the greatest change in the way people live? What changes can you identify as having been caused by the invention?

"Return With Us, Now, To Those Thrilling Days of Yesteryear . . ."

Episodes of the *Lone Ranger* were popular on radio in the 1930s and 1940s and on television from the late 1940s to the early 1960s.

People who grew up during the first few years of television still get shivers up and down their spines when they hear or see the phrase, "Return with us, now, to those thrilling days of yesteryear." Though it may sound silly to say so, for those who first saw him on the black and white television sets of the late 1940s and early 1950s, there will always be a Lone Ranger.

Since it began, television has been a popular form of entertainment and information. People take their television programs seriously. They talk about television in positive and negative terms.

Some of the talk about television takes the form of debate between those who approve of television and those who feel its effects are mainly harmful. Those who like television and those who dislike television agree on one point: *Television influences the way people think, the way they feel, and the way they behave.* Today we are just beginning to understand how growing up with television has changed our lives.

The title of the next section is probably familiar to most students. It is something parents have been saying about television ever since its invention. In this section, one of the authors of this book looks back at his first introduction to television during the late 1940s.

"Turn That Thing Off!"

When I think back to 1948-61, the period between my fifth and eighteenth birthdays, my most frequent memory is my mother's almost constant command: "Turn that thing off!" She had remarkable hearing. No matter where she was and no matter how devious I was, she could always tell when I had turned on the television.

When I arrived home from school, I would slip into the living room and carefully turn on the set. I was certain that my mother could not hear the barely audible sound of the Lone Ranger as he spoke with his faithful Indian companion, Tonto. Nevertheless, no matter how careful I had been, my mother would call from the basement where she was doing laundry or from the attic where she was storing winter clothing: "Turn that thing off!"

When I was eleven, my mother took a job in a local dress shop as a salesperson. She would often call home after school to give me instructions about warming the oven or putting out the garbage. If I was watching television, I would always carefully turn down the volume before I answered the telephone. But my mother's hearing was extraordinary. No matter how careful I had been, she would always end her instructions with the familiar command to "turn that thing off!"

Our first television set was a floor model or console which occupied considerable space in our small living room. The cabinet was walnut veneer. The speaker was covered with fabric that had strands of gold thread running through it at regular intervals. The screen was about forty-three centimetres measured diagonally. When the set was off, the screen had a grey-green cast to its surface. This wasn't a very attractive colour to most people, but it was almost my favourite. My favourites were black and white, the "colours" which played across the surface of the television screen when it was on! When the set had been on for a

The first televisions, such as the one shown here, cost several months' income.

while and someone turned it off, the black and white picture would collapse into a white dot in the middle of the screen. After a few seconds, the white dot would disappear and the surface of the screen would return to its grey-green colour.

The first sets in our community sold for about $650, if you could get one. The average monthly wage in 1948 was approximately $200. If my family had had to buy our first set, we would have had to dig into the family savings or perhaps wait for some time until we had gathered together enough money.

As it turned out, the first television set in our house was a gift! My sister had been dating a fellow who was pretty well off. He bought us the set as an act of generosity or perhaps as a bribe to persuade my mother to allow him to marry my sister.

Our first set came with a small indoor antenna called rabbit ears. It was called a rabbit ears antenna because it had two antenna that looked vaguely like the ears of a rabbit to people who had never seen a rabbit. In any event, the rabbit ears antenna wasn't good enough to capture the signals from the stations south of the border in the United States.

Canada didn't have its own stations at the time we got our first television. As a result, we had to erect a hefty antenna on the roof next to the chimney. My sister's boy friend hadn't counted on this as part of the bargain. He didn't mind the expense, but he didn't particularly like high places. For the better part of one weekend, he wrestled with the tubular metal structure while I shouted instructions about the reception through the living room window. "Whoa, that's better. No. No! Whoops! Take it back the other way a bit. No! No! I mean the *other* way!"

Soon the antenna was in place and working with some regularity. Now, we could get channels from across the border in the United States. The first shows I watched were *Roller Derby* and *Wrestling. Roller Derby* is a sport where teams of roller skaters try to knock one another over in order to be the first to get to the finish line. It might have been a popular sport in the United States where people didn't have a chance to see hockey played well, but for many Canadians it was pretty dull.

This first experience with television didn't prevent me from becoming a regular viewer. It wasn't long before I was watching *Hopalong Cassidy, Gene Autry*, and the *Lone Ranger* on a regular basis.

During the early days of television, my mother was not a fan. Looking back, I think two factors account for her reservations about television in our home. The first reservation was connected to the use of the living room as a place for watching television.

Before television, our family's living room, like many Canadians', was one of the least used rooms in the house. The living

Before the beginning of cable service, television antennae filled the skyline of most Canadian communities.

room was for visiting relatives or special guests. We hardly ever spent time there. As a result, the chesterfield in the living room had little wear. Even though it was almost ten years old when we got our first television set, the family chesterfield looked as if it were new.

As soon as television arrived in our living room, it became painfully obvious to my mother that the materials used to cover living room chesterfields would have to be far sturdier than they used to be to withstand the more constant use.

The other thing that caused my mother to have reservations about television was the articles she read in magazines from the United States. Soon after my sister's boy friend had installed the antenna for our set, my mother came home from the store armed with proof of television's negative effects. According to my mother, television would lower our cultural tastes, make me into a juvenile delinquent, create moral depravity in our community, and ruin my eyesight.

Not once during those early years of television did my mother bring home an article in favour of television. I didn't know it then, but, for each of the articles my mother brought home about the negative effects of television, there was another telling about television's positive consequences. According to these articles, television would help to expose sin and corruption, enhance our freedom of speech, bring culture to millions in their own living rooms, provide tired workers with entertainment at the end of a long day, and increase our standard of living by promoting the consumption of new goods and services.

I didn't realize it at first, but television had begun to change our lives. At first, the changes were small, but they became more significant as time went on.

Before our first television arrived, we had been fans of radio. My mother listened to the radio regularly and frequently. She turned the radio on in the morning when she went to the kitchen and rarely turned it off during the day, unless she went shopping.

After the arrival of television, we listened less to the radio, relying more on television for information about the world in which we lived.

We saw on television things we would have never known about from radio. For example, we were a family of hockey fans. We listened regularly to Foster Hewitt broadcast the games from Maple Leaf Gardens in Toronto, Ontario. We were faithful listeners, hanging on his every word. No matter who the Maple Leafs played, the opposition always played roughly, making the Leafs' struggle seem more valiant and pure.

Television changed all that. Television proved to us that, for all those years on the radio, Foster Hewitt had embroidered the truth. Television revealed that our beloved Leafs played as roughly as the opposition. What our ears could not detect from the radio was revealed by the unblinking eye of the television camera!

Our lost innocence about the way the Leafs played hockey was accompanied by other subtle changes in our lifestyle. Before we

From the 1920s to the 1950s radio was the most popular home entertainment medium.

received our first television set, our Saturday routine was the same week after week. Each Saturday morning, we would do a regular set of chores, changing the sheets on the bed, vacuuming, washing the kitchen floor and scrubbing the bathroom. When these chores were completed, my sister and I would go shopping with a list our mother had carefully prepared the evening before.

While we shopped, our mother did the laundry and prepared lunch. Our arrival home was always greeted with an inquiry about what we had forgotten. When the groceries had been put away, we would all sit down to lunch.

After lunch, my sister would take me to the local library to pick out books for the week. We would then go to a movie. Or more precisely, we would attend a Saturday matinee. We were often accompanied by one of my sister's boy friends.

The matinees almost always consisted of several cartoons followed by a "serial" and "feature." A serial was a short movie about a villain placing an innocent victim in grave danger. Just when the situation looked worst for the victim, the movie would end. This forced us to return the following week to see if the hero would be able to rescue the victim before disaster struck.

Although the changes were slow, our family patterns began to change. Eventually, I was more and more reluctant to join my sister on the shopping expeditions. It isn't clear whether it was the attraction of the television or my increasing maturity that made me want to stay at home on Saturday mornings, but stay at home I did.

Gradually my mother, too, became a fan of television. It began with the hockey games on Saturday night and gradually extended to other programs. By the time Canadian television was flourishing in the 1950s, my mother was a regular viewer. She enjoyed *Front Page Challenge*, a popular quiz program, and *Country Hoedown*, an entertainment program featuring Tommy Hunter.

I didn't much care for the early CBC dramatic programs my

CBC programs of the 1950s, such as *Front Page Challenge*, were broadcast live.

mother watched. To a twelve-year-old, the first CBC dramas had two problems. For one thing they were more like plays than movies. The actors bellowed out their lines as if they were talking in front of an audience. They didn't seem to know that they were on television and that television was different from a play.

Another problem with early CBC drama for a twelve-year-old was the plays themselves. Many of these early plays didn't seem to have definite endings. As a twelve-year-old who had read every Hardy Boy mystery in the local library, I found the absence of a definite conclusion to a story extremely irritating. In most of the stories I read, good triumphed over evil. The CBC plays were different and confusing. You often weren't sure how things turned out in the CBC plays.

Television drama changed along with television itself. And, as television changed, it also became apparent that television was changing us, too. It was probably this that made my mother so

■ **Investigation 2.1:** | *To Evaluate Why People Watch Television*

Method:

1. Write a paragraph in which you explain the reason or reasons you watch television.

2. Make a list of all the reasons the members of your class have for watching television. Discuss the range of responses made by class members.

   a. What is the most common reason given for watching television?

   b. Do you think there are "good" and "poor" reasons for television viewing?

3. Interview adults about their reasons for watching television. Compare their responses to those of students in the class. If there are differences between the reasons provided by adults and those provided by your classmates, attempt to explain the differences.

4. Make a list of the programs you watch during a two- or three-day period. Refer to the paragraph you wrote in which you stated your reasons for watching television. Did the programs you watched satisfy the reasons you had for watching television?

5. Studies indicate that once a channel is selected, the majority of viewers continue to watch that channel, regardless of the programs being shown. What does this reveal about the reasons people have for watching television?

6. Is there a relationship between the amount of television people watch and the reasons they view television? For example, do people who watch larger amounts of television have different purposes for watching than people who view less television? What are the implications of your findings for the variety of programs offered on television?

Skills Developed: 1.21; 1.22; 1.23; 1.24; 1.25; 2.6; 3.2; 4.2; 4.3; 4.4

cautious about television. She recognized television's power to change things. She had recognized the strains that television would put on our living room furniture and she could cope with them. But would she be able to cope with the less apparent and less tangible changes that television would bring to our lifestyle?

Canada At Mid-century

By 1945, when the Second World War finally ended, Canadians were war-weary. They entered the postwar period eager to put the memories of the war years and the hardships they had suffered behind them.

The war had made unprecedented demands on Canadians. Many died in the war and many others were injured. In addition to the personal losses suffered by many families, almost no person in the country had been untouched by the financial difficulties caused first by the Great Depression and then by the war.

During the 1930s and 1940s, economic hardship had become a way of life for the majority of Canadians. The financial difficulties which had begun during the Great Depression of the 1930s were continued during the war so that the production of military supplies could be maintained. For a period of more than fifteen years, the average Canadian had come to know economic privation personally.

The end of the Second World War marked the end of economic and personal suffering for many Canadians. As industry returned to producing civilian products, many Canadians found a new prosperity. The availability of goods and services increased dramatically. From butter to automobiles, the Canadian consumer seemed to have found a commercial utopia!

As Canada entered the 1950s, it was becoming clear that patterns established during previous generations were changing. For young people, growing up during the 1950s was very different from the way that their parents grew up during the 1930s.

Excerpt from Eaton's *Fall and Winter Catalogue*, 1932-33.

Growing up during the 1930s meant living with economic hardship in a country that was dominated by people who could trace their origins to Britain. Anglo-Celtic traditions were the strongest in the lives of most of Canada's people. A main link binding Canada's people together from coast to coast was the Eaton's catalogue. Both French- and English-speaking Canadians obtained many of their possessions by selecting them from its pages. The images on the pages of the catalogue were mainly rural. Canadian literature and art also reflected Canada's vast rural landscape and concerns about survival in a harsh, natural environment.

Much, if not all, of that changed during the 1950s. Canadians saw the building of highrise apartments and office buildings in their largest cities. Stalled by the depression and the Second World War, construction in Canada's urban centres exploded during the 1950s.

The automobiles that began to choke city streets took many Canadians to their first suburban homes. Canada's urban building boom spilled over into the countryside where developers created "gracious suburban homesteads."

The dominant culture at the beginning of the 1950s was white, Anglo-Saxon, and Protestant. The addition of more than 1 500 000 immigrants during the following decade began to change the image Canadians had of themselves. Though most of the immigration to Canada was from European countries and from the United Kingdom, Canada's population was becoming increasingly diverse. Communities of Italians, Hungarians and Ukrainians began to establish themselves in Canada's urban centres.

Although it seems modest by today's standards, the average weekly industrial salary in 1950 was $45.08. At mid-century, Canadians had a sense of affluence that hadn't existed during the preceding generation. This sense of prosperity continued throughout the decade. The gross national product, the value of all the goods and services produced in Canada, climbed from $18 billion per year to more than $36 billion by the end of the decade.

Prosperity meant the ability to acquire consumer goods from automobiles and automatic washing machines to electric can openers and TV dinners. In 1955, it was claimed that there were more than 100 varieties of TV dinners. Served in foil containers, TV dinners consisted of foodstuffs which brought tears to the eyes of home economists.

During the 1950s, Canadians bought more cars, built more homes and had more babies than in any previous decade. Young males of the early 1950s wore pants which were baggy at the knees and narrow at the ankle. They grew their hair long on the sides and cut it short on top. They combed it into what was supposed to resemble a duck's tail. Many young women wore their hair in ponytails, wore saddle shoes and bobbysocks, and had their ears pierced for the wearing of earrings.

There was rock n' roll music. Paul Anka sang about "Diana,"

■ **Investigation 2.2:**

To Determine The Accuracy Of The Way That Television Presents The Past

Method:

1. Select a television drama that uses an historical setting.

2. Using newspapers, magazines, history textbooks, journals and diaries, attempt to answer the question: To what extent does television present an accurate reflection of the past?

3. Prepare a set of notes which will help both to defend and to refute the position: *When television presents the past, it often presents a distorted picture of what actually happened.*

Skills Developed: **2.2; 3.4; 4.1; 4.5**

the Diamonds sang "Little Darlin'," and the Crewcuts sang "Sha Boom." The Rock n' roll of the period featured a background of meaningless sounds that became known as "doo-wop" because that was the main background lyric!

Test Yourself

A. *True and False:* Indicate with the letter T or the letter F whether you think the following statements are accurate or inaccurate. If any part of the statement is false or inaccurate, use the letter F.

1. The first appearance of television in Canada was during the Second World War.

2. During the 1950s, Canadians enjoyed far greater prosperity than they had known during the previous twenty years.

3. Canadian society in the 1950s was predominantly white, Anglo-Saxon, and Protestant.

4. Made cautious by years of depression and war, Canadians purchased few consumer goods during the 1950s.

5. The vast majority of articles that dealt with television during the 1950s were critical of the new medium.

B. *Activities for Further Investigation*

1. This chapter describes how the televising of hockey games made fans aware that radio accounts of the games had not been entirely accurate. Today, television is the medium most people use to learn about events. It is the window through which people see their world. Write a one-page essay about the following statement: "Seeing is believing."

2. People hold strong views about television. Some call television a "boob tube," implying that there is little programming that challenges people to think. In an essay, comment about the amount of intellectually challenging material available on television.

3. According to the authors of this text "television has influenced the way people think, the way they feel and the way they behave." How much influence has television had on you? Write a brief essay about the influence of television on the way you think, feel and behave.

4. What makes television a popular medium? Is it the easy access people have to television? Is it the excitement that television dramatic programming provides? Is it television's ability to bring people up to date about the world in which they live? Do heavy viewers (20 or more hours per week) and light viewers (less than 10 hours of viewing per week) give the same reasons for watching television?

Construct a questionnaire to tap people's reasons for watching television and the amount of viewing they do per week. Administer the questionnaire in your neighbourhood, put the results together in a table, and present them in a brief essay.

5. In an essay, describe how television fits into your lifestyle. Explain when and why you watch television and its relation to your other activities. Has your pattern of viewing always been the same or was your pattern different when you were younger?

Television in Canada

The Early Years

During the late 1940s and early 1950s, those people in southern Ontario who had television sets picked up signals from stations in the United States. By 1951, there were almost 40 000 television receivers in southeastern Ontario picking up signals from the stations south of the border. In 1952, the first stations were established in Canada by the Canadian Broadcasting Corporation (CBC). They were located in Montreal and Toronto.

Within about ten years time, almost 110 Canadian stations served approximately 87% of all Canadian homes that had television. By 1962, there were 4 000 000 homes with television sets in Canada. In that year, the average Canadian viewer spent almost five and one-half hours watching programs each day.

Table 3.1: *Canadian Households with Television, Selected Years, 1953-1981*

Year	Percent of Households With		Total Percent
	One TV	*Two or More TV Sets*	
1953	10.2	....	10.2
1956	53.6	....	53.6
1961	80.2	4.0	84.2
1965	81.8	10.9	92.7
1969	76.0	20.0	96.0
1975	65.0	31.8	96.8
1981	59.8	40.1	99.9

Source: Statistics Canada

A number of factors influenced the rapid spread of television and made its acceptance easy. The technology for television had already been developed before the beginning of the Second World War. The problems of **signal transmission** and **reception** had been worked out even before the first sets were sold in Canada. Although the process was by no means as good as it is today, television in the late 1940s was free of major technical problems.

Television was also able to spread rapidly because society had patterns into which television easily fit. War production had stalled the spread of such devices as washing machines, toasters and record players. After the war, industry could return to the production of such goods, and people began to look forward to larger numbers of such labour-saving devices.

People were used to listening to the radio and seeing motion pictures on a regular basis. The presentation of sound and pictures together was familiar to anyone who had gone to a movie theatre. The adjustment to the presentation of sound and pictures in the home was relatively easy.

The Canadian government had already worked out a structure for controlling radio which was easily applied to television. The Broadcasting Act of 1936, passed by Parliament, had given the Board of Governors of the Canadian Broadcasting Corporation the authority to operate a national broadcasting service and to regulate the operations of broadcasting networks and stations.

Canada's first English-language television broadcast, on September 8, 1952, was less dramatic than one might have expected. The first broadcast began with a test pattern. The test pattern was followed by a drawing of an Indian which some observers insist was shown upside down. Television's first broadcast of program length was a children's show called *Uncle Chichimus*, starring a chubby, bald-headed puppet.

Percy Saltzman has the distinction of being the first English-speaking Canadian to appear on Canadian television. From the

This Indian head test pattern was an early CBC logo.

Percy Saltzman's weather report was the first program broadcast on English-language television in Canada.

CBC's Toronto studio, Mr. Saltzman's image was broadcast to 10 000 living rooms. His subject was the day's weather!

Although its beginning wasn't dramatic, in the years that followed, television would change almost every aspect of Canadian life — its politics, economics, social relations and the ideas the people held. Among the first changes that could be observed was television's seemingly magnetic ability to attract people's attention. Almost regardless of program content, people found the illuminated screen of a television set fascinating.

People rearranged the furniture in their living rooms to make room for their new television set. The first sets were large by today's standards and took up considerable space. When neighbours visited, people pointed with pride to the new set and motioned the visitors into chairs and chesterfields to share the new viewing experience.

Television's popularity increased quickly. By 1954, there were more than 1 000 000 sets in use in the country. Some Canadians had become familiar with television before its formal introduction to Canada in 1952. As many as four years before the first CBC broadcast, Canadians living in southern Ontario were able to tune in American television programs broadcast from stations south of the Canadian border.

Well before Percy Saltzman stepped in front of the television camera, Canadians had become familiar with American comedian Milton Berle ("Uncle Milty"), Ed Sullivan, Gorgeous George, the Roller Derby and the Lone Ranger. Canada's close proximity to the United States meant that, from the outset, Canadians would be as familiar with American media figures as they would be with their own.

Television in Canada might have begun fourteen years earlier than it did. In 1938, the CBC made the first application for a private television station. However, it was not until 1948 that the

Table 3.2: *A Comparison of Television Broadcasting and Use in Canada and the United States, 1980*

	Canada	United States
POPULATION AND HOUSEHOLDS		
Population	23 745 000	220 100 000
Total Households	7 728 000	77 900 000
Television Households	7 504 000	76 300 000
STATIONS AND SYSTEMS		
Originating TV Stations	111	1 011
Cable Systems	562	4 225
TELEVISION RECEIVERS (% of Total)		
Television Households	97%	98%
Multi-set TV Households	37%	50%
Colour TV Households	78%	83%
Cable TV Households	54%	21%
TELEVISION VIEWING (Hours: Minutes)		
Average Daily Household Viewing	5:29	7:05
Weekly Viewing	22:38	27:24
Men	26:41	33:14
Women	21:38	23:55
13-19 year old Children	19:12	25:59

Source: CRTC *Facts Digest on Broadcasting and Telecommunications in Canada*, December 1980

NOTE: This comparison provides general guidelines only. Information may differ from other sources quoted in this book because the methods of gathering information and times of collecting the information were different from the other sources.

Corporation asked the government for funds to begin the project. The CBC received government approval to build stations in Montreal and Toronto in 1949.

By 1952, the Toronto and Montreal stations were operating. A year later, Vancouver and Ottawa stations began operation for the CBC, and in 1954 Halifax and Winnipeg began service. Ten years later there were 110 stations operating in Canada, serving 87% of all Canadian homes with television.

The Canadian System Of Broadcasting

Canada's system for television broadcasting combines public and private ownership. Within the public sector, the Canadian Broadcasting Corporation (CBC) is the lawfully established "national broadcasting service." Under the terms of the 1968 Broadcasting Act, the CBC is charged with the responsibility of providing a service which should:

- be mainly Canadian in content and character, helping to develop national unity and the expression of Canadian identity;

- provide information, enlightenment and entertainment for a population with diverse interests and tastes in both English and French; and

- serve the various and different needs of Canada's regions by contributing to the exchange of cultural and regional information and entertainment.

Its special responsibilities and sources of revenue give the CBC a unique place within the structure of broadcasting in Canada.

The CBC owns and operates 900 of the 1900 stations, transmitters and production centres located in Canada. It is associated with another 400 privately or community-owned facilities which are CBC **affiliates**. The remaining 600 broadcasting facilities are local, independent broadcasters, privately owned commercial networks like CTV, or provincially owned educational television facilities.

The CBC is a Crown corporation established by Parliament on November 2, 1936. The Broadcasting Act of 1936 gave the CBC the right to control private broadcasting in Canada as well as public broadcasting. In 1958, a new Broadcasting Act created the Board of Broadcast Governors which was given responsibility for regulating both public and private broadcasting in Canada.

Ten years later, the Board of Broadcast Governors was replaced by a new regulatory body, the Canadian Radio-Television Commission. This body was given the responsibility for licencing and

CBLT Toronto on the first broadcast day for English-language television, September 8, 1952. *Left to right: standing* — Jim Ellis, Tom Null, Bill Brady, Mavor Moore; *seated at control panel* — Gordon Shillabeer, Drew Crossan, Valerie Carson, Vic Ferry; *foreground* — Bill Andrews, Garry Lee.

regulating all Canadian broadcasting. In 1976, the CRTC's responsibilities were extended, giving it the power to regulate federally controlled **telecommunications carriers**. Today, the CRTC is officially called the Canadian Radio-television and Telecommunications Commission.

Although the CBC is financed mostly from funds provided by the federal government, its special position under the Broadcasting Act allows it to operate independently of government management. Other Crown corporations are the responsibility of a minister of the government and come under that minister's direct control. The CBC is unusual in this respect. It must report on its spending to Parliament each year through the Secretary of State, but it is not responsible to either that minister or to the government for carrying out its activities.

The Canadian people through Parliament provide most of the money the CBC needs for its operations. In 1980-1, CBC expenses requiring Parliamentary monies amounted to $531.1 million for **operating costs** and $48.5 million for **capital costs**. Additional funds, in the form of paid advertising on its television stations, provided income of $131.5 million to the Corporation. Another $9.9 million in income was obtained from other sources such as the sale of programs to foreign broadcasts.

In 1983, the CBC spent more than $750 million for all of its operations. Of the total expenses of the Corporation, the CBC spent approximately $500 million for its French- and English-language television services. This figure is the equivalent of approximately $20.00 for each Canadian.

Television coverage on the CBC reflects its mandate as a national broadcasting service. It provides program material which includes popular entertainment, music, drama, children's programs, current affairs, news reporting and analysis, history, religion, art, science, agriculture, sports, consumer affairs, community information and special events.

Of the content presented on the CBC in recent years, approximately 70% has been of Canadian origin. CRTC regulations require 60% Canadian content during **prime time** between 6:00 p.m. and midnight. Private television stations are required by the CRTC to provide 50% Canadian content during prime time and 60% Canadian content overall.

CBC programs are distributed across the country to Canada's six time zones by approximately 88 000 km of **microwave network** and by **Anik** satellite. Since 1973, the CBC has leased channels on the *Anik* satellites which are owned and operated by Telesat Canada.

CBC television programs are fed to the satellites from CBC control centres in Toronto (English) and Montreal (French) as well as from other CBC centres when it is necessary. The signals are sent to the satellites from the control centres and are received back from the satellites in CBC's main regional centres. The regional centres add local programs and redistribute the programs by microwave to **rebroadcast transmitters** in their area or province. In the North, satellite television service is sent directly to isolated transmitters operated by the Corporation.

Canada Pioneers In The Use Of Satellites

On July 1, 1958, the Canadian Broadcasting Corporation televised a special program to celebrate the opening of coast-to-coast microwave transmission service. With a network stretching from Victoria, British Columbia, to Sydney, Nova Scotia, Canada could boast that it had the largest television network in the world. A year later, when the line across the Cabot Strait to Newfoundland was completed, Canada had a 6 400 km long microwave network linking one coast with the other.

Almost as soon as the microwave network had been completed,

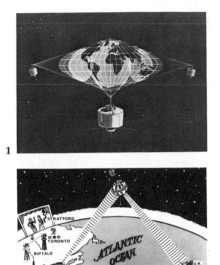

1 This drawing shows how three geosynchronous satellites can provide uninterrupted television service to the entire globe.

2 The drawing illustrates the transmission of a television program from Stratford, Ontario, to England via Telestar satellite.

CBC engineers began to think about a space satellite system. They knew that, as good as it was, the microwave network would eventually be limited. It took almost a decade to form a corporation to develop, own and operate a satellite system in Canada. By 1969, The Telesat Corporation (now Telesat Canada) had been formed to begin construction of a Canadian communications satellite.

In November 1972, the *Anik A1* satellite was launched. This satellite, which took its name from the Inuktitut word for "brother," was a satellite that maintained a **geosynchronous** orbit. Geosynchronous means that the satellite orbits in a way that allows it to maintain its position in relation to the earth's surface. This allows signals from the satellite to reach Canada from coast-to-coast between the 39th parallel and 80°N.

In another ten years time, Canada had developed the need for additional types of satellites with expanded coverage and strength. By the early 1980s, Canada had established itself as a world leader in the development and use of satellites for **telecommunications**.

Experimentation with different uses and forms of satellite communication has been part of the Canadian legacy. Satellites have been used for two-way communication in connection with educational and medical services. Using programs of the Ontario Educational Communications Authority, the CBC and the British Columbia Television System, investigations of direct-to-home broadcasting by satellite have also been conducted.

The Inuit Tapirisat of Canada have conducted some unique experiments with the *Anik B* satellite system. Using ground stations at Frobisher Bay, Pond Inlet, Igloolik, Baker Lake, Eskimo Point and Cambridge Bay, the Inuit have used the satellite for transmitting television messages from one community to another. The messages took the form of workshops, lessons and meetings.

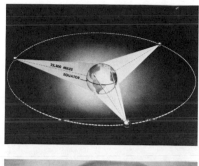

3

4

3 Telestar satellite depicted in orbit. (22 300 miles = 35 887 km)

4 Andover Horn, a 54 m tracking antenna for receiving signals from satellites.

Work such as these experiments conducted by the Inuit has placed Canada at the forefront of experimentation with satellite systems.

Two-way Television

Until the 1980s, communication using television was mainly a one-way experience. Viewers could receive messages from the various systems to which their television sets were attached, but they could not respond to the information. Toward the end of the 1970s and the beginning of the 1980s, television began to become a two-way phenomenon.

Each year, larger and larger numbers of people throughout North America are using their television sets as part of a large two-way communications network. The range of uses is potentially limitless. It is already possible to order goods and services seen on television simply by pushing a button on a device that looks like a pocket calculator

People can use their televisions to gain access to large data storage banks. These banks hold information about many different items from airline timetables and lists of good wines to video games and statistical programs for performing complicated mathematical operations.

People regularly read news information by calling it onto their television screens. Those who wish printed copies of the material they are reading can get it with the aid of a home **microcomputer** and a printer.

Systems linking television sets with large computerized data banks are called **teletext** or teletex. Canada is a pioneer in teletext technology, manufacturing Telidon terminals. Telidon is a device about the size of a pocket calculator that permits the user to use his or her television to communicate with data banks. The British

Telidon is one of the most sophisticated videotex systems in the world. Researched and developed in Canada, it has been adopted by many of the world's largest communications companies. With Telidon, a home television set can be turned into a powerful information centre and bring electronic shopping and banking right to the user's fingertips. The diagram, based on a drawing in *This Is Telidon* published by Canada's Department of External Affairs, shows some typical Telidon system components and accessories:
1. Large screen projector system.
2. Cassette storage device.   3. Digitalizing tablet with electronic stylus.   4. Computer monitor.
5. Image creation system.
6. Floppy diskette.   7. Modified TV set or colour monitor.   8. Decoder.   9. Keyboard.   10. Joystick.

have developed a similar system called Prestel. The French system is called Antiope.

In addition to Telidon-like devices, people use home computers to link their television sets with data storage systems. If their microcomputers are connected to a printer, they can make a permanent copy of the material they call up on their sets by giving their microcomputers the appropriate commands.

The quantity of information, games and specialized services available to consumers is increasing at a rapid rate. Already users can get French vocabulary drills, poker and arcade-style games, airline schedules, political reports, lists of ski resorts, sports news, the weather, and about one thousand other items. People can get access to these items by connecting a microcomputer and television set to a data storage bank.

Two-way television systems and computerized data retrieval systems are costly. There is growing concern in Canada that people may be denied access to information and opportunities to learn because they cannot afford to pay for such services. For example, imagine that two high school students are given an identical assignment to investigate the economic system of a particular country. One student with access to a microcomputer is able to use the most recent information from commercially available data banks. The other, a less affluent student, is limited to the resources of the school and public libraries.

Storing Television Images And Sound

The development of video-cassettes and video-discs for the storage of pictures and sounds is also changing how people use television in their homes. Commercially available pre-recorded cassettes and discs allow people to rent or purchase programs and playback devices for use at times convenient to them. People who have video-cassette recorders in their homes can record television programs for later viewing or create their own programs with the addition of a television camera.

The Betamovie, a video camera and video-cassette recorder combined in one package, makes shooting your own video movies simple.

Beginning with feature-length movies, the use of video-cassettes and video-discs expanded rapidly after their introduction during the 1970s. Any audio-visual or text material can be recorded on video-cassettes or discs, including film, filmstrips, slides, microfilms and printed materials from books, magazines, newspapers and computer printouts. By the 1980s, the range of material that was available was limited only by the costs of production and purchase.

Used in connection with microcomputers, video storage technologies are expanding educational possibilities dramatically. People using microcomputers coupled to video storage are able to obtain a far wider range of material than they could in a single classroom or school. By controlling the pace, complexity and order of the material students study, what and how students learn can be made more varied and given greater depth than ever before.

Pay Television Comes To Canada

On March 18, 1982, the nature of Canadian broadcast television changed. That day, the Canadian Radio-television and Telecommunications Commission announced that it was granting licences to four regional and two national **pay-television** operators for a five-year period. The pay-television operators were licensed to charge a monthly fee for permitting people to view the programs offered.

Pay television had already been well developed in the United States at the time of the CRTC decision. The profitable experience of pay television in the United States had encouraged Canadian pay-television operators because of the potentially large profits to be made in Canada.

Canada is the most heavily **cabled** country in the world. Canadian entrepreneurs reasoned that very large profits could be made by providing a pay-television service using existing cable facilities. Pay-television applicants reasoned that subscribers would pay between $75 and $250 per year for specialized programming. However, in less than a year, the regional channel specializing in cultural programming had gone bankrupt, and a major reorganization of the surviving cable companies was already being considered.

The licencing announcement of the CRTC was seen by many as the beginning of a new era for Canadian television. Anticipating new, high quality programs, many people enthusiastically applauded the Commission's decision.

Critics of the decision, however, wondered whether pay television would be able to make good its promise of better quality

---

■ **Investigation 3.1:** *An Inquiry Into Public Attitudes Toward Pay Television*

Method:
1. Administer a questionnaire similar to Appendix II, "Public Attitudes Toward Pay Television," to a sample of people living in your community.

2. Organize your data to permit you to compare the responses of those who subscribe to pay television, those who no longer subscribe to pay television, and those who have never subscribed to pay television.

3. What similarities and differences do you find among the responses of the three groups? Are the heaviest viewers of television among the subscribers to pay television or are they among the viewers of commercial/public television? What attracts people to subscribe to pay television and what stops others from subscribing?

4. Present your findings to the class, commenting about the general reactions to pay television by members of your community.

Skills Developed: **1.22; 1.26; 2.7; 3.4; 4.2; 4.3; 4.4; 4.6**

---

programming. These critics feared that pay television would simply spread existing programming over more television services. This, they felt, would water down television's quality.

By making all of the pay television licences expire on March 1, 1987, the CRTC seemed determined to maintain control over the pay-television operators. The limitation on the licencing period was applauded by people who wanted to make sure that pay-television operators lived up to the requirements of their licences.

Licences established terms and conditions of operation for

pay-television stations. For example, one of the national operators, First Choice, was granted a licence to provide two services,
one French and one English, each for twenty-four hours per week.
About 70% of the programming was to be first-run movies of
feature length and 30% was to be specials. During the first three
years of its licence, First Choice was expected to deliver at least
30% Canadian content. During the remaining two years of its
licence, First Choice was required to provide 50% Canadian content.

Table 3.3: *A Chronology of Television and Television-Related
Technologies*

1924	V.K. Zworikin, a Russian-American inventor, makes application for a patent for a television camera pickup tube (iconoscope).
1925	J.L. Baird demonstrates television in Britain.
1928	J.L. Baird demonstrates colour television (Britain).
1929	The Bell Laboratories (U.S.) experiment with colour television.
1932	BBC (England) takes over the responsibility for developing television from the Baird Company.
1933	Philo Farnsworth develops electronic television.
1936	Britain begins regular television service.
1938	20 000 television sets are in service in New York City.
1939	United States begins regular television service.
1942	The first electronic brain/automatic computer is developed in the United States. Magnetic recording tape is invented.
1945	Rapid expansion of television in United States with spillover "coverage" in Canadian border areas such as southern Ontario.

1946	The ENIAC computer is completed and demonstrated at the University of Pennsylvania.
1947	Bell Laboratory's scientists (Schokley, Britlain, and Bardeen) invent the transistor.
1949	Canadian government announces interim television plans and authorizes the CBC to establish stations and production centres in Toronto and Montreal.
1950	1.5 million television sets are in use in United States.
1951	40 000 television receivers in Canadian homes are receiving programs from the United States.
	15 million television sets are in use in the United States.
1952	Canadian government announces policy for a general system of television with a CBC-owned station and production centre in each of the main regions.
	CBFT Montreal opens on September 6, 1952, and CBLT Toronto on September 8, 1952, offering about 18 hours of programming per week in both English (CBLT) and French (CBFT). CBFT and CBLT can reach about 30% of all Canadian homes, more than have television receivers.
1953	By January, programming in Canada is 30 hours per week. A microwave link between Buffalo, N.Y., and Toronto makes it possible to carry programs from the United States "live."
	By May, microwave circuits joining Toronto, Montreal, and Ottawa are established.
	June 2, CBOT (Ottawa) begins service in time to cover the coronation of Queen Elizabeth II.
	By fall, new private stations begin to come onto the air. October 20, CKSO-TV (Sudbury) becomes the first private television station to go on air in Canada.
	December, CBUT (Vancouver) becomes the fourth CBC station on the air.
	First telecast from Canadian House of Commons featuring the visit of U.S. President Eisenhower.

Thousands of Canadians purchased their first television to view the coronation of Queen Elizabeth II on June 2, 1953.

Microwave television tower.

1954	CBMT (Montreal) provides English service to Montreal and CBFT becomes a full-French service. CBWT (Winnipeg) and CBHT (Halifax) open.
	1 000 000 Canadians own television sets.
	29 million U.S. homes have television sets.
1955	Commercial television begins broadcasting in Britain.
	CBC telecast of the Opening of Parliament.
1956	Bell Telephone begins development of a "visual telephone."
1957	USSR launches *Sputnik I* and *II*, the first earth satellites.
1958	60 Canadian television stations are in operation with a coast-to-coast microwave network spanning more than 6 400 km.
	U.S. artificial earth satellite *Explorer I* is launched from Cape Canaveral, Florida.
1959	Television coverage of British General Election.
1960	U.S. launches a radio-reflection satellite.
	Optical microwave laser is constructed.
	Television sets: United States — 85 million
	Britain — 10.5 million
	Canada — 3.5 million
	West Germany — 2 million
	France — 1.5 million
1961	CTV network opens in October with microwave transmission linking Vancouver, Calgary, Winnipeg, Edmonton, Toronto, Ottawa, Montreal and Halifax.
1962	CBC participates in carrying global satellite transmission from *Telstar* relay on July 23.
	Advertisers spend $90 million for television advertising in Canada.
	More than 85% of all Canadian homes have at least one television set.
1966	September 1, first regular colour programming in Canada.
	U.S. spacecraft *Surveyor I* transmits more than 11 000 television images of the moon's terrain.

1967	April 27, CBC telecast of the official opening of Expo 67 via space satellite.
	June, first taped television service to Yellowknife, N.W.T., begins.
1968	First televised national debate among Canadian political party leaders (Trudeau, Stanfield, Douglas, Cauette) by CTV and CBC on June 9. Audience: 9 million viewers.
	Intelsat 3A, the first of a new series of Canadian communication satellites is launched.
1969	Telesat Corporation (Telesat Canada) formed to construct world's first geosynchronous orbit satellite.
1970	Canadian content regulations are announced by Canadian Radio-television and Telecommunications Commission.
	231 million television sets are estimated to be in use worldwide.
1971	Television is admitted to regular proceedings of Nova Scotia Legislature for a three-week experimental period.
	INTEL develops first microprocessor, paving the way for microcomputers.
1972	House of Commons (Ottawa) committee approves in principle the admission of television to sittings of Parliament.
	Anik A1, Canada's first domestic communications satellite, is launched from Cape Canaveral, Florida.
	Question period is broadcast from House of Commons (Ottawa).
1974	January, Global Television Network airs officially.
1975	Television cameras are admitted experimentally to the proceedings of a Canadian Senate committee, Legal and Constitutional Committee, discussing a bill about marijuana.
	CBC removes all commercials from television programs directed to children 12 years of age and younger.
1976	Television is admitted on an experimental basis to regular proceedings of Ontario Legislature.
1977	Personal computers, designed for home use, are marketed.

1979	Personal computers provide colour graphics using a television set.
1982	CRTC announces that pay-television licences have been granted to Canadian operators.
1984	Canadian Broadcasting Corporation provides exclusive coverage of Pope John Paul II's Canadian visit. Canadian Broadcasting Corporation budget of $900 million reduced by $75 million, prompting reconsideration of its mandate.

Factors Affecting The Acceptance Of Television In Canada

The easy acceptance and rapid spread of television during the 1950s was helped by several factors. Television's technology had been developed and tested long before sets were made available for public purchase. In Britain and the United States, television technology had been operating during the 1930s. Thus, by the time television was introduced in Canada in 1952, most of the technical problems had been successfully solved.

By 1952, Canada had a well-established broadcasting technology into which television could easily fit. The CBC had been established as a national radio broadcasting service. The addition of television to the CBC's service presented no special difficulties.

The provision of funds by Parliament for the establishment of the CBC's television facilities enabled television to develop in a secure financial atmosphere. Given Canada's vast landscape and small population, private Canadian corporations were not interested in developing television in Canada at that time.

The necessary regulations to control broadcasting had been developed for radio. The addition of television within the Canadian regulatory structure was easily accomplished. Later, that

People's familiarity with radio and movies made Canadians' acceptance of television easy.

structure was changed to accommodate the changing nature of television and Canadian society.

More important than any of the preceding factors was the readiness of Canadians for change. The transition from the depression and the Second World War to a peacetime society set the stage for many new developments in Canadian society. Television was simply one of the changes for which Canadians were ready.

Analysts studying the conditions affecting changes within a society have found that changes in a society's technological structure are more likely to occur than changes in its value structure.

Television was just such a technological change. Its introduction into Canada did not demand that people change how or what they thought. Television's influence on values and beliefs was subtle and was not well understood. At the time of its introduction, television appeared to be simply another technological development like the washing machine or automobile.

Analysts have also observed that change is more likely in areas for which there are roughly similar substitutes. While there are some fundamental differences between television and motion pictures, there was sufficient similarity to insure that people would not be threatened by the new technology.

Changes also occur more frequently in the external form things take than in their substance. Television changed the form of information by adding pictures to words and presenting them to people in their homes.

Television did not really change the substance of what was presented. People were seeing on television the same themes, people and events that they were used to seeing in the movies or hearing on radio. The dramatic form of television plays followed formulas developed 2 000 years earlier by the Greeks.

The technology of television and its content were easily handled by Canadians. Manipulation of a few knobs and minor adjustments to antennas did not prove to be very difficult. The people, events, and themes presented on television were familiar. They did not seriously challenge people's ways of thinking or their values. In short, television was a friendly addition to the Canadian family.

Test Yourself

A. *Identification:* Explain the meaning and/or significance of the following in your own words.

Broadcasting Act

Canadian identity

affiliate

prime time

Board of Broadcast Governors

Telesat Corporation

Telidon

Canadian Broadcasting
  Corporation

Canadian Radio-television and
  Telecommunications
  Commission (CRTC)

public ownership

private ownership

Crown corporation

Anik

microwave

pay television

cable television

teletext

B. *True and False:* With the letter T or the letter F indicate whether you think the following statements are accurate or inaccurate. If any part of the statement is false or inaccurate, use the letter F.

1. A society's technological structure is easier to change than its value system.

2. The average Canadian watches more television each week than the average American.

3. In the years immediately after the Second World War, Canadians proved reluctant to accept new forms of technology.

4. Women watch more television than men.

5. Canada is a world leader in satellite television technology.

6. Privately owned television stations in Canada are exempt from Canadian content regulations.

7. The CBC is directly controlled by the Minister of Communications.

8. The advent of television in Canada forced the Canadian government to develop an entirely new regulatory agency for the new technology.

9. Early television viewers were attracted to television with little apparent concern for the content of programs.

10. Many Canadians were suspicious about the potential impact of television during the early years of the medium.

C. *Multiple Choice:* For each question, indicate the response you think best answers the question.

1. Television technology was developed to a commercially acceptable level by 1938. However, in Canada it was not until 1952 that the first television broadcasting facilities were established. The delay between the development of the technology in Canada and the establishment of a television network was due to:

   a. government reluctance to grant licences.
   b. economic difficulties caused by the Great Depression.
   c. the problems caused by the Second World War.
   d. the absence of Canadian business people willing to take a risk on the new technology.

2. The largest portion of funding for the CBC comes from:
   a. money provided by the Canadian Parliament.
   b. the sale of advertising time on television.
   c. private donations by individuals and private corporations.
   d. revenue from cable and pay television.

3. Opposition to pay television came mainly from people concerned that:
   a. pay television would make outrageous profits.
   b. the quality of television programming would be watered down.
   c. pay-television operators would not be bound by Canadian content regulations.
   d. Canadians would be unable to pay the monthly subscription fees for pay-television services.

4. The CBC expenditures for 1981 were:
   a. under $100 million.
   b. $500 million.
   c. $700 million.
   d. $1 billion.

5. In 1983 the CBC cost the average Canadian:
   a. $150 annually.
   b. $75 annually.
   c. $5 annually.
   d. $20 annually.

6. A geosynchronous satellite:
   a. receives a signal from a transmitter.
   b. orbits in a way that allows it to maintain its position in relation to the earth's surface.
   c. is used for two-way television transmissions.
   d. passes over Canadian territory four times daily.

7. The CRTC requires that the CBC play at least:
   a. 60% Canadian content in prime time.
   b. 80% Canadian content in prime time.
   c. 25% Canadian content in prime time.
   d. 50% Canadian content in prime time.

8. Prime time refers to the period in the broadcast day:
   a. between noon and 10:00 p.m.
   b. between 10:00 a.m. and 10:00 p.m.
   c. between 6:00 a.m. and midnight.
   d. between 6:00 p.m. and midnight.

9. Which of the following is more common in Canada than in any other country?
   a. Cable television service
   b. Pay television service
   c. Two-way television
   d. Satellite dishes

10. Which of the following factors does NOT explain why television was accepted readily by most Canadians soon after its introduction?
   a. People were used to radio and motion pictures.
   b. People saw in television an escape from the difficulties in their lives.
   c. Canadians were eager for new technology and labour-saving devices.
   d. Long-established regulatory agencies were able to control the impact of television in Canadian society.

D. *Activities For Further Investigation*
1. The CRTC denied licences to pay-television operators until March 1982, years after pay television had become established in the United States. The delay was due to many concerns.

Among these were fears that pay television would not add significantly to the quality of existing television fare and that the success of pay television would undermine the quality of free, public television. In an essay, weigh the benefits and the problems caused by the spread of pay television in Canada.

2. The development of television technology, particularly satellite transmission of television signals, has enabled television to reach areas of Canada previously too remote for television service. While the extension of television service has long been a target for the CRTC, many critics have expressed concern that the advent of television in northern, native communities has had a most harmful effect. Investigate the impact of television on native communities (native Indian and Inuit) in Canada. What have been the advantages and disadvantages of the coming of television to these areas of Canada?

3. With the development of videotape and other related technologies, television is playing an expanded role in public education. Write an essay commenting on the following statement: "Television monitors will replace teachers in the classroom in the school of the future."

4. The development of two-way television has been greeted by two main reactions. Some have welcomed it as an advancement that will greatly aid its users in performing many daily activities. They praise the tremendously increased access to information it promises for its subscribers. Others claim it will bring unprecedented dangers, particularly in the area of invasion of privacy. Investigate two-way television and write an essay considering the possible benefits and dangers of this technology.

5. When approval was given for the development of a television network in Canada in 1949, it was decided that television

should be a publicly owned and operated enterprise. From 1952 until 1961, when the privately owned CTV network was licenced, television in Canada remained a public enterprise. In the United States, television was first developed by private corporations with public television (Public Broadcasting System) following much later.

In an essay, explain why Canadian regulatory agencies chose to establish a public television system first. Indicate whether you believe this decision helped or hindered the development of television in Canada.

Television Viewing:
The Human Dimension

The Blind Men And The Elephant

Many, many years ago, there lived six elderly blind men. Each day after his chores were completed, a young man would visit the six blind men, offering aid and friendship.

On one occasion, the old men asked their young friend if he would lead them to the centre of the village where they could sit, enjoying the sounds of village activity. "Certainly," replied the young man. "I will take you tomorrow, as soon as I have finished my chores."

On the following afternoon, the blind men waited eagerly at the door of their house for their friend. The young man finally arrived. "I have not finished my work, but I will take you to the village now and return for you when my chores are done."

After he had taken them to the village, the young man departed to complete his work. The six blind men soon grew tired of sitting in the village square, and decided to move cautiously around the square. They formed a line. By placing their right hand on the shoulder of the man in front, each was able to follow the other.

Growing bolder with each step, the blind man at the head of the line walked more and more quickly toward the edge of the square. The men then snaked around the square's edge. The procession stopped abruptly when the first man walked into the side of an elephant. The momentum of the others propelled them in several directions around the elephant.

"Ouch," exclaimed the leader, "I have walked into a wall!"

By this time, the others were reaching out to find their companions. As they did, each man touched a different part of the elephant.

One man screamed as he touched the elephant's trunk, thinking it was a huge snake. Another, grasping the elephant's ear, thought he had taken hold of a large fan.

"Ouch," said another, touching the pointed end of the elephant's tusk.

The two remaining blind men found the elephant's leg and tail. The one who had taken hold of the elephant's leg thought he had found a tree trunk. The other who took hold of the elephant's tail was certain he had found a rope.

The elephant's driver shouted at the blind men, frightening them. "Release that elephant, you old fools!"

When they were reunited, the blind men began to talk about their experience. "An elephant is a wall," said one. "I am certain, because I have never bumped into anything so large and flat until today."

"No, no," insisted another. "An elephant is a snake. I have held it in my hand, I know."

In no time at all, the blind men were fiercely arguing. Each man was certain that the elephant was something different.

"Wall."

"Snake."

"Spear."

"Rope."

"Fan."

"Tree."

The young man, returning from his chores, could not help overhearing the argument among his blind friends. "You are all wrong," he said. "Each of you has touched a different part of the elephant. You must combine your experiences to find the truth."

With the dispute settled, the young man took his friends back to their home.

Viewing Television: The Human Dimension

You know, a picture doesn't lie. I know that and you know that. That is why television is such an enormously effective medium. But while a picture doesn't lie, a picture may not tell all the truth.

RICHARD M. NIXON, President of the United States

Just as the blind men disagreed about the elephant, people differ in their perceptions of television programming. What people see on television and how they respond to what they see depends on many different influences. Among the strongest is the viewer's previous experiences. The same television program may be viewed very differently by people who have had different experiences.

A wide range of influences shape people's experiences and ideas, including such elements as age, education, group memberships, and political outlook. These elements become the filters through which people see the world in which they live, including television.

It is obvious, for example, that young children and people in their teens do not see things in the same way. Young children's mental abilities are not as developed as those of older people. This difference affects what young children and older people see on television.

Young children have more difficulty than older children knowing where a program ends and a commercial message begins. Older children are more capable of distinguishing what is "real" from what is "fictional" than younger children.

Education is an important influence on what people see and how they interpret what they see. For example, students who are familiar with the techniques of television production are better able to understand how certain illusions are created for the viewer than are students who have not learned about such techniques.

The groups to which people belong also help to shape their responses to the world around them. People identify more closely with the outlooks of the groups to which they belong.

Young people are more likely to view a television program about rock n' roll music than are senior citizens. Senior citizens, on the other hand, would probably be more interested in watching a television program about the problems of living in retirement communities.

People belong to many other groups in addition to their age group. Canadians who are active members of the Roman Catholic Church are more likely to seek information about changes in Catholic Church policy than are people of other religious backgrounds. Torontonians would be more interested in changes in Ontario's tax laws than people living in Vancouver. In general, people seek out messages that match their own ideas and avoid information that contradicts their viewpoints.

What people see and how they respond to what they see on television is influenced as much by their own experiences as by what is actually shown and how it is presented. Like the blind men exploring the elephant, people must combine a variety of sources of information to get a complete picture of the television experience.

It would be a mistake, however, to minimize the impact of television's content and techniques on the viewer. The selection of television content and the way it is organized and presented influence what the viewers see and how they react to what they see.

The Unblinking Eye: The Television Camera

Camera Angles

The television camera is the viewer's eyes, shaping what the viewer sees and the viewer's reactions to the scene. The camera provides the viewer with an image and suggests to the viewer how to interpret the image presented. Camera angles and the types of lenses used on the camera affect the viewer's understanding of what is being seen.

A raised eyebrow, an inflection of the voice, a caustic remark dropped in the middle of a broadcast can raise doubts in a million minds about the veracity of a public official or the wisdom of a government policy.

SPIRO AGNEW, Vice-President of the United States

The typical way a person sees a scene is at eye level. This is called a **normal-camera angle**; it shows the world as a person normally sees it. The content must be taken into account when considering what is "normal." Viewing preschool children from an adult's normal angle of vision would be different from viewing the preschoolers as children their own size would normally see them.

A normal-camera angle depends upon the subject's position. If the subject is seated during an interview, the normal angle is at the subject's eye level. If the same subject stands up, the camera would be raised to eye level to produce a normally angled shot of the subject.

A camera positioned above the subject's eye level, looking down on the subject, is called a **high-camera angle**. This viewpoint is often used to give the viewer a broad look at the scene.

High-camera angles influence how the viewer sees the subject. A high angle makes the subject appear smaller than it would appear if a normal-camera angle was used. When viewers look down on a subject from high-camera angles, the subject often looks lonely and less powerful than when viewed from a normal angle.

When the camera is positioned below the subject's eye level, the angle is called a **low-camera angle**. Viewed from this perspective, a subject looks larger and more powerful than when viewed from a normal-camera angle.

Advertisers use low-camera angles to enhance the viewer's impression of the product being advertised. Automobiles are often photographed using a low-camera angle. This makes the car look longer and more powerful than it would look if it was seen from a normal-camera angle. Advertisers often use low-camera angles to make children's toys seem larger and more exciting to the viewer.

Low-camera angles are sometimes used in producing political

High-camera angle.

Low-camera angle.

■ Investigation 4.1:

To Recognize How Close-ups Affect The Message And Emotional Tone Of A Picture

Method:

1. Select a series of large photographs from a variety of magazines.

2. Place an L-shaped piece of black cardboard on the pictures to create different pictures and emotional reactions.

3. Develop a brief explanation of the way close-ups alter the meaning and emotional reaction people get from the pictures they see.

Skills Developed: **3.2; 4.3; 4.4**

campaign commercials. When a political candidate is viewed from a camera angle slightly below normal, viewers are given the impression that the candidate is taller and more powerful than is actually the case.

Investigation 4.2: *Testing The Influence Of Low-, Normal- And High-camera Angles On Viewers' Reactions To A Television Production*

Method:

1. With the cooperation of the school's administration, invite a speaker to prepare a five to fifteen minute lecture about a topic of interest to students.

2. Explain to the speaker the purpose of the experiment.

3. Prepare three videotapes at the same time. Arrange three cameras along the same vertical axis. Place one at a high angle, one at a normal angle and one at a low angle.

4. When the tapes have been prepared, *randomly* assign students from another class to each of the three groups or conditions: low-, normal- and high-camera angle.

Random assignment of students to groups in an investigation is an important way of avoiding bias. If students picked the condition they preferred, students with similar points of view might all be assigned to the same group. Because a person's point of view affects how he or she sees and interprets events, it is desirable to make certain that people with similar points of view are present in about the same proportion in all experimental groups. In this way biases are equally distributed across all conditions of the study and will not affect the results.

Random assignment can be accomplished by putting each student's name on a piece of paper. Place the names of all the students in a bowl or hat. First, draw a name for the *normal condition*, a name for the *high condition* and a name for the *low condition*. Continue until all of the names have been assigned to a viewpoint.

5. Tell the students that they have been selected to evaluate a

speaker's suitability for addressing the whole student body on the topic for which the speaker was invited.

6. Show one group the videotape which shows the speaker from the low-camera angle. Show the second group the videotape which shows the speaker from a normal angle. And show the third group the tape which shows the speaker from a high-camera angle. Keep the groups separated until the experiment has been completed. This will help to avoid confusing the results because the students will not have discussed what they have seen and their reactions.

7. Immediately after each tape has been shown, give each student in each group a reaction ballot similar to Appendix III at the back of the book.

8. After the three groups have seen the tapes and completed the reaction ballots, tabulate the responses on a tabulation sheet similar to Appendix IV.

9. Examine the tabulation carefully. Write a general statement about the relation between what the viewers saw and their reactions to what they saw. *How does the angle from which a speaker is viewed influence the viewers' reactions to the speaker?*

Skills Developed: **3.1; 3.2; 4.3; 4.4; 4.6**

The viewer can be made to feel that a scene is suspenseful, exciting or unreal by tilting the camera, disturbing the normal horizontal planes. The tilted or **canted angle** is most easily produced with a portable camera. On studio cameras, the effect is produced by using a prism which is fitted over the lens of the camera. When the prism is turned, the image is tilted to produce the canted angle which gives the scene its unusual quality.

The camera can be positioned so it seems that it is a character involved in the action, showing the viewer how the scene looks from the character's point of view. This is called a **subjective camera angle** or a **point-of-view shot**. Some action/adventure programs make effective use of the subjective camera angle.

Shooting a scene with a portable camera from the viewpoint of one of the participants can create tension and excitement. For example, picture a scene in which two young children are being chased by some unknown creature through a densely wooded forest. The subjective camera is running through the bush as if it was one of the children.

Branches strike the camera's lens as if they are striking the child's face. The tired child begins to run more slowly. By making the camera plunge toward the ground, the "child" seems to stumble. Using the subjective camera angle, the viewer is brought into the scene as an active participant.

Shooting a scene from CBC's 1983 production of *Backstretch* on location, using a mobile crane.

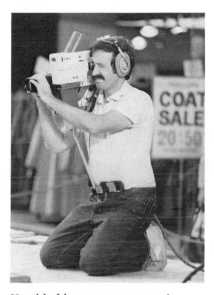

Hand-held cameras are much more mobile than the cumbersome cameras of the early years of television.

Camera Lenses

The viewer's perception of a scene is affected by the choice of lens placed on the camera as well as by the camera angle. In the same way that changing the lens of a microscope affects how and what people see, changing camera lenses affects how a scene is viewed and what is seen.

Although there are many types of lenses, three distinctions will help to show the relation between lens choice and viewing. A **normal-angle lens** creates an image similar to what a person's eye sees. The relation between the subject on which the camera is focussed and objects in front and behind the subject appear as they would to the eyes. The size of objects, their depth and speed of movement all appear normal.

Wide-angle lenses give the viewer a very broad view of a scene, but there is little magnification of the scene or objects in it. In fact, when wide-angle lenses are used, it is often difficult to pick out details in a scene because the scene is so broad.

Wide-angle lenses are used when it is desirable to exaggerate the impression of depth, distance and/or speed of movement in a scene. Wide-angle lenses are often used to show the movement of trains across the prairie landscape. Movement is easy to follow because the view of the scene is broad, but the appearance of moving objects is distorted.

As they move, objects seem to grow in size or get smaller very quickly. This occurs because the lens distorts the relation between objects near to the camera and those far away. Objects nearer to the camera appear much larger than objects in the background. Thus, an object moving toward the camera almost seems to leap at the viewer.

These properties — exaggeration, depth, distance and the speed of movement — make the wide-angle lens useful. A wide-angle lens is used when someone wants (a) to make a scene look larger than it is, (b) to make objects near to the camera appear more powerful than they are, and/or (c) to create the illusion of speed. Advertisers who want to exaggerate the length of automobiles and their apparent speed use a wide-angle lens at a low-camera angle. This combination creates the impression that the car is sleek, streamlined, powerful and fast.

Impressions opposite to those obtained by using a wide-angle lens can be created by using a **narrow-angle** or **telephoto lens**. The narrow-angle lens makes objects in a scene (a) seem closer together than they really are, (b) appear to be about the same size and (c) move at a very slow rate of speed.

The narrow-angle lens magnifies subjects and appears to flatten their features. Because distances between objects appear compressed and the size of objects are made to appear more equal, moving objects seem to have their speed reduced.

In a track and field event, for example, sprinters racing toward a camera using a narrow-angle lens seem to be moving very slowly. It appears as if they were on a track moving in the opposite direction. They struggle and strain, but their progress toward the ribbon at the finish line is slow.

Editing

In television, sounds and pictures are combined to produce an impact on the viewer. If the message being delivered by the sound portion matches the visual message being delivered by the picture, the impact on viewers will be different than if the picture and sound images do not match.

The process of assembling the sound and picture material for presentation to the viewer is called **editing**. Editing involves three basic processes — shot selection, timing, and movement from one shot to another.

This is a 1984 set for *The Wayne and Shuster Show*. Wayne and Shuster have starred on Canadian television since its beginning.

Shot Selection

Today, most television production involves the use of film or videotape which can be manipulated (edited) after the images have been recorded. However, even when production doesn't involve film or videotape, editing is a factor.

Investigation 4.3: *How Editing Affects The Communication Of Information*

Method:

1. Collect two or three magazine pictures, measuring at least 12.5 cm by 17.5 cm.

2. Using strips of construction paper, construct an "adjustable frame." Use this frame to reduce or "crop" the size of the area of the photograph which is visible.

3. Compare the cropped image of the photograph with the original. Has the meaning of the photograph changed? What information provided in the original is not evident in the cropped photograph? Does the information in the cropped photograph take on a new meaning when compared to the uncropped picture? Deliberately try to create a different or "weighted" meaning by cropping the photograph in a particular way. Is it difficult to do this? How many different effects can you achieve?

4. Discuss the following statement: *What you do not see in a photograph may be as important or more important than what you do see.* Consider the implications of your investigation for the fair and the accurate presentation of news using photographic images.

Skills Developed: 1.11; 1.22; 1.23; 2.2; 3.4; 3.5

This is the control room for CBC's *The Journal*. Each camera shooting has a monitor screen. The people in the booth have the job of switching cameras for varied shots without causing breaks in the show.

With live broadcasts involving more than one camera, the director decides which shots will be used. The editorial decisions of the director during a live broadcast affect what the viewers see and how they respond.

The order in which material is presented to the viewer has a significant impact on the viewer's reaction. An experiment performed more than sixty years ago shows how people are affected by the arrangement of shots.

Using a movie camera, the experimenters photographed a male actor with a neutral expression on his face, a bowl of soup, a small child playing, and an old woman lying in a coffin. They then created three different photographic sequences. In one, the photographs of the soup appeared between shots of the male actor. In the second, the footage of the child playing was placed between photographs of the male actor. And, in the third, a shot of the coffin was placed between the shots of the actor.

Table 4.1: *Experimental Shot Sequences*

Sequence	First Shot	Second Shot	Third Shot
One	Actor	Soup	Actor
Two	Actor	Child	Actor
Three	Actor	Coffin	Actor

The three sequences were shown to different audiences. Those who saw the first sequence thought the actor looked especially hungry. Viewers of the second sequence said that the man's love for the child, whom they thought was his daughter, was very great. The third sequence prompted comments about the sadness that the man must have felt at the death of the woman.

In each case, the audience mentally related what were, in fact, unrelated shots. In other words, the viewers created patterns and gave the patterns meaning, they made sense out of what they saw. This illustrates the impact that the order of material can have on viewers.

■ **Investigation 4.4:** *Testing The Influence Of Shot Sequence On Viewers*

Method:

1. Begin by preparing three shot sequences, using videotape recording equipment if it is available. If it is not available, use photographs presented as slides or stills. Each sequence should begin and end with identical shots of the same material such as a person with a neutral facial expression.

Insert between the beginning and ending shots in each sequence another shot of equal length. Use different middle shots for each of the sequences.

For the inserted shots use subjects with no apparent connection to the beginning and ending shots. Using subjects that are very different for each sequence is most effective.

2. Separate each sequence from the others on a videotape and label each sequence with an identification number.

3. Arrange to randomly divide students in another classroom into three groups.

4. Tell the students that they have been picked to preview one of three experimental productions. Show each group of students the sequence to which they have been assigned. Keep the groups separated until the experiment has been completed. This will help to avoid confusing the results because students will not have had the chance to discuss what they have seen.

5. Immediately after the sequence has been shown to each group, give each student in the group a reaction ballot similar to Appendix III.

6.   After the three groups have seen the sequences and completed the reaction ballots, tabulate the responses on a tabulation sheet similar to Appendix IV.

7.   Examine the tabulation sheet carefully. Describe the main response to each of the three sequences at the bottom of the tabulation sheet.

8.   Write a general statement about the connection between sequencing shots and the meaning viewers give to the sequences they see. *Do different sequences of unrelated shots prompt different reactions from viewers?*

Skills Developed: **3.1; 3.2; 4.3; 4.4; 4.6**

Timing and Transitions Between Shots

Other important elements in television production are the length of time each shot appears and the speed of the changes between shots. These two production elements also affect the viewer's impression of a program.

In a televised variety show involving a singer performing a slow-moving ballad, shots of the singer would remain on the screen for relatively long periods of time. The movement from one shot to another would occur calmly in keeping with the tempo of the song being sung.

In a dramatic program featuring a heated argument between two characters, the timing of the shots would reflect the mounting tension between the characters. Shots of one person and then the other would alternate rapidly, adding to the tension between them.

At the climax of the argument, one person might strike the other. The camera would probably focus on the reaction of the person (a reaction shot) who had been struck, maintaining that shot longer than the ones leading up to that point in the action. Holding a reaction shot gives emphasis to the action the viewer has just seen.

Rapid movement from shot to shot creates tension in the viewer when the material is familiar. When the material is unfamiliar, rapid movement from one shot to another can cause confusion in the viewer. This can be an effective technique when the purpose is to puzzle the viewer, increasing the mysteriousness of the production.

Changes or transitions from one shot to another can be accomplished in four ways: cutting, fading, dissolving and wiping. Each technique has different uses and produces different results for the viewer.

Investigation 4.5:	*To Consider The Emotions That Television Programs Attempt To Evoke In The Viewer And The Ways That These Emotions Are Evoked*
Method:	1. Human emotions cover a very wide range, including such feelings as happiness, sadness, anger, fear, delight, vengeance, tension, boredom, excitement, regret, empathy, guilt, interest, concern, suspicion, confusion, nervousness, calm. 2. Select one television program that arouses one of these feelings in you. In a paragraph or brief essay, describe your reaction fully and explain how the program you selected succeeds in conveying the emotion. Among the methods you should consider are characterization, plot development, lighting, stage and set design, and camera techniques.
Skills Developed:	1.14; 1.15; 1.22; 1.23; 1.24; 1.26; 2.3; 3.1

The **cut** is the most common and the most rapid way to change from one shot to another. Cuts occur instantly, like the blinking of an eye.

The **fade** is accomplished in two basic ways. A *fade-in* involves moving from a black screen to an image. A *fade-out* occurs in the opposite manner, turning from an image to a black screen.

Fades are used to separate program segments much as a curtain is used to signal the end of one act and the beginning of another in a play. When a major change in location or time period is called for, the fade is the transitional device most often used to indicate the change. Because the speed of a fade can be controlled, it can be used to give emphasis to an event, allowing the viewers to think about what they have seen.

A third transitional device, the **dissolve**, involves blending one visual image into another. It is produced by simultaneously fading in one shot and fading out another. The speed of dissolves can be controlled, allowing for smooth transitions between shots.

An early CBC Toronto studio with a boom microphone.

Television productions of orchestral music and ballets typically use dissolves to make smooth flowing changes between one shot and the next.

The most obvious and abrupt transitional device is the **wipe**. In a wipe, a new picture wipes across the screen replacing the previous shot. Because wipes are obvious and abrupt, they are sometimes used to indicate changes in location or time which the director wants to make very obvious to the viewer.

Editors play an immensely important role in the production of television programs. Through their efforts, unwieldly amounts of material are made to fit coherently into a specific time slot. Through techniques such as cuts, dissolves and the placement of images in relation to one another, the editor helps determine the impact of the film on the viewer.

Television's Impact On What Viewers See

When people are first introduced to one another, they search for clues about the qualities their new acquaintance possesses. People assess new acquaintances by noting the style and condition of the person's clothing, his or her posture and gestures, whether the person smiles easily, and a wide variety of other factors.

Knowing that viewers are attentive to small visual cues about a person's personality, those responsible for the costumes and make-up worn by performers pay close attention to detail. They try to make viewers believe that the performer is genuinely the sort of person that he or she is paid to present.

When a program is first created, the writers usually try to take their mental picture of a character and change it into a recipe which can be used to select suitable performers. They state how the performers should look, how they should dress and be made up, and how they should behave.

Bruno Gerussi's character, Nick
Adonidas, is the hero of *The
Beachcombers*.

Marc and Susan Strange created the idea for the CBC drama
The Beachcombers, which was first shown in 1972. They had a
mental picture of the leading character, Nick Adonidas, which
was expressed in a written description. They described Nick as
" . . . about 40, wiry and swarthy with a thick mane of black hair
turning silver at the temples. . . . There is something about him
of the pirate, something of the poet . . . totally free and living by
his wits. The key to Nick is that he is passionate, vital and in love
with life . . ."

Along with information contained in specific scripts, this description was used as a basis for casting Bruno Gerussi in the
role of Nick. It was used to decide what Bruno Gerussi would
wear and how he would act out the part of Nick Adonidas.

The statement "don't judge a book by its cover" is a warning
that first impressions may be misleading. People are not always
what they at first seem. In fact, a number of television programs
have created misleading first impressions for viewers as a way of
fooling them about a character.

Another old phrase, "a wolf in sheep's clothing," refers to situations where someone who is dangerous, like a wolf, is presented as someone who is gentle and kindly, like a sheep. It is
also possible to present sheep looking like wolves. Paramount's
Happy Days uses the deliberate contrast between Fonzie's appearance and his real character in exactly this way. Fonzie looks
and talks tough, but acts gently.

In some forms of television programming, the performer's character is not considered important. News and public affairs programs, for example, want the viewers to think of performers as
neutral observers. The idea is that the viewer's judgement of the
message being delivered shouldn't be influenced by the person
delivering the message. Nevertheless, investigators have conducted a number of studies which show how television techniques may affect the viewers' perception of news, current affairs,
and educational programming.

In one study, investigators compared two televised lectures in which all features were identical except one. The only visible difference was that in one situation the audience could see that the lecturer was using notes. In the other situation viewers could not see the use of notes. Those viewers who saw the lecturer use notes thought that the lecturer was less fair and less straight-forward than the viewers who saw the same lecture but could not detect the use of notes.

In order to avoid this problem, newscasters often use **tele-prompting** or **autocuing devices** which allow performers to read scripted material without it appearing that they are reading. This is accomplished by projecting the printed material in the region of the camera's lens. By projecting the material in this region, the newscaster appears to be looking at the camera's lens while reading from the teleprompting device.

Visual interest in news programs is often maintained by combining photographic material with the image of the performer who is presenting the news. This is accomplished by an electronic process called **keying** or **chromakeying**. Using two cameras, one for the performer and one for the photograph, the illusion that the performer is positioned in front of the photograph is created for the viewer.

A study comparing the use of a plain background and a picture background produced some interesting results. Using the format of a newscast, one audience saw a performer read a news story with a background picture. Another audience saw the same performer read the same story in front of a plain background. The audience which saw the newscast with the picture background thought the performer was more believable than the audience which saw the identical newscast with the plain background.

On news broadcasts, reporters are sometimes photographed from the front and sometimes photographed from the side, showing the speaker's profile. Interestingly, the angle — front view or profile — influences the viewer's evaluations of the reporter.

■ **Investigation 4.6:** *Testing The Influence On Viewers Of Front Versus Profile View Of A Speaker*

Method: 1. With the cooperation of the school's administration, invite a speaker to prepare a five to fifteen minute lecture about a topic of interest to students.

2. Explain to the speaker the purpose of the experiment.

3. Prepare two videotape recordings at the same time. Place one camera directly in front of the speaker at a normal-camera angle, obtaining a shot of the speaker's head and shoulders. Place the other camera at a right angle to the first, framing the shot in the same way.

4. Randomly assign students from another class to each of the two conditions: *front* and *profile* view.

5. Tell the students that they have been selected to evaluate a speaker's suitability for addressing the whole student body on the topic for which the speaker was invited.

6. Show one group the videotape which shows the front view of the speaker. Show the other group the videotape which shows the profile view of the speaker.

7. Immediately after each tape has been shown, give each student a reaction ballot similar to Appendix III.

8. After the two groups have seen the tapes and have completed the reaction ballots, tabulate the responses on a tabulation sheet similar to Appendix IV.

9. Examine the tabulation sheet carefully. Write a general statement about the relation between what the viewers saw and their reactions to what they saw. *How does the front versus profile view of a speaker influence the viewer?*

Skills Developed: **3.1; 3.2; 4.3; 4.4; 4.6**

CBC film editor Harry Workmeister at work.

Two groups of viewers were shown the same newscast. One group saw the reporter from the front as the reporter read from a teleprompting device and appeared to be looking directly at the camera. Another group saw the identical newscast, but shown from the half-profile point of view. In this situation, the reporter appeared to be taking part in a discussion. When the reporter appeared in the half-profile position, he got better ratings for reliability and expertise than he did when viewed from the front.

One interpretation of these results makes an interesting point about television broadcasting. It illustrates that, when experts are shown on television, they are often being interviewed and shown from the side. People are accustomed to seeing experts in profile. Thus, when a news reader is shown in profile, the audience tends to associate that camera position with expertise. In other words, the camera position seems to add to the reliability and expertise of the performer, even when the coverage remains the same.

Much of television's impact on the viewer is produced by editing techniques. One study investigated the effect of cutting between shots of a lecturer's presentation and shots of the studio audience's reaction to the lecture and lecturer.

Two identical tapes were created. Positive audience reactions were cut or edited into one tape of the lecture. Negative audience reactions were cut into the other. Investigators weren't surprised to find that the tape containing positive audience reactions produced more favourable viewer reactions than the tape containing negative audience reactions.

It has become commonplace in television productions to insert additional applause or laughter in some program content, especially in entertainment programming. This practice, sometimes called "sweetening the sound track," is used to increase the program's appeal to the viewer.

The step from sweetening the sound track to enhancing viewer interest by inserting favourable audience reactions isn't very big.

Including favourable audience responses in political broadcasts or campaign material may create more positive viewer responses than might normally occur. If no audience reactions were presented and the viewers were allowed to evaluate the broadcasts themselves, they might respond less favourably.

Investigation 4.7:

To Identify And Evaluate The Impact That Sounds Have On What People See On Television

Method:

1. Cover the television screen with dark coloured paper or adjust the brightness control knob until the picture disappears. Listen to a ten- to fifteen-minute segment of a program.

2. Write a brief paragraph summarizing the events that took place while the visual images were hidden.

3. Discuss how the following sound features contributed to your impressions of the program:
a. volume
b. tone
c. music

4. If the program you watched is available on videotape, review the program with the screen images. How accurate were your impressions when you relied only on what you heard?

5. Before television, people listened to drama and comedy on the radio. Obtain a recording of a radio drama and listen to it with your classmates. Compare the use of sound on radio with the use of sound on television.

6. Select a two- to three-minute sequence from a television drama or movie that is available on videotape.

7. Play the sequence for the class without the accompanying sound track.

8. Using a tape recorder, compose a sound track to accompany the sequence.

9. Play the original and student-made sound tracks along with the sequence.

10. In class, discuss the different impact produced by the original and student-produced sound tracks.

Skills Developed: **1.11; 1.22; 1.23; 1.25; 1.26; 2.2; 3.2**

Test Yourself

A. *Identification:* Explain the meaning and/or significance of the following in your own words.

normal-camera angle	high-camera angle
low-camera angle	canted-camera angle
normal-angle lens	wide-angle lens
telephoto (narrow-angle) lens	editing
cutting	fading
dissolving	wiping
keying (chromakeying)	teleprompter

B. *True and False:* Indicate with the letter T or the letter F whether you think the following statements are accurate or inaccurate. If any part of the statement is false or inaccurate, use the letter F.

1. Young children have difficulty distinguishing real from imaginary events shown on television.

2. Students who learn how television works are better able to understand what they see than students who do not learn how television works.

3. People prefer watching programs about people who are different from themselves.

4. Camera angles can influence a viewer's impression of the honesty and ability of a news reporter.

5. Live telecasts cannot be edited.

6. Rapid movement from shot to shot can create a feeling of tension and confusion in the mind of the viewers.

7. Newscasters who use teleprompting devices are fairer and more expert than those who do not use such devices.

8. Very young children usually prefer commercials to regular programming.

9. A television character's appearance and personality must always be compatible.

10. Adding laughter or applause to a sound track can increase the appeal of a program to a viewer.

C. *Multiple Choice:*   For each question, indicate the response you think best answers the question.

1. The use of a high-camera angle tends to make a subject look:
   a. powerful.
   b. intelligent.
   c. frightened.
   d. powerless.

2. A director wishing to film a sports car for an advertisement would likely use:
   a. a normal-camera angle.
   b. a low-camera angle.
   c. a high-camera angle.
   d. a canted-camera angle.

3. The technique which is used to show the viewer the world as seen by the characters is:
   a. a subjective camera angle.
   b. a low-camera angle.
   c. an objective camera angle.
   d. a canted-camera angle.

4. If a director wishes to make objects in the foreground appear larger than they really are, he or she will use:
   a. a normal lens.
   b. a telephoto lens.
   c. a wide-angle lens.
   d. a prism.

5. A canted angle:
   a. is often used for close-up shots.
   b. makes distant objects appear closer than they are.
   c. distorts the horizontal plane of the picture.
   d. makes the viewer see exactly what the character is seeing.

6. Which of the following is *not* a function of the editing process?
   a. shot selection.
   b. selection of the camera angle.
   c. length of time spent on one shot.
   d. movement from one picture to another.

7. If an editor wished to depict the passage of time from one shot to another, he or she would most likely use a:
   a. fade.   **c.** wipe.
   b. cut.   **d.** dissolve.

8. Which of the following devices would be most effective in showing events happening at the same time?
   a. fade.   **c.** wipe.
   b. cut.   **d.** dissolve.

9. Sweetening a sound track refers to:
  a. the use of mood-enhancing music to evoke viewer response.
  b. the use of an added laugh or applause track.
  c. varying the sound volume to produce a desired effect.
  d. panning the audience to show smiling audience faces.

D. *Activities For Further Investigation*

1. It was noted in this chapter that young children often have difficulty telling the difference between real and imaginary scenes shown on television. After watching a Saturday morning's programming, write an essay commenting on the problems presented to viewers of these programs. Do you think that the makers of the programs you watched take into account the fact that their viewers confuse the real and the imaginary on television?

2. Which of the following people do you believe plays the most important role in the production of a television program: the script writer, the camera operator, or the editor? State your reasons for making the selection you did.

3. Select your favourite character from television. Write a summary of the character's physical and behavioural characteristics. Identify the reasons that you find the character appealing.

4. Comment about the following statement: "Much of television production involves an attempt to manipulate the response of the viewers."

5

How A Television Program Is Made

Making television programs is a complicated and costly business. The production of a television program depends on many people. Each person involved has a responsibility to ensure that the program meets the artistic and financial standards set by the **producer**. The producer oversees the entire production process, paying particular attention to the financial aspects of the project.

A television production typically begins with an idea or **program concept** in the mind of a producer or someone who has presented the idea to the producer. A program cannot exist unless the producer agrees that the idea is worth doing.

Among the first tasks the producer performs is to plan a **production budget**. In the budget, the producer anticipates all the costs of making the program. No matter how good the idea is, if the budget is more than the amount of money the producer has or can get, the program will not be made.

If the producer can count on sufficient financial support for the program, a **writer** or writers will be hired to develop a **script** or format. The first form a script takes is often a detailed **sequence outline**.

In a sequence outline, the writer takes the program concept and translates it into words. The sequence outline describes the sequence of action from the beginning of the program until the program has ended.

If the producer likes the sequence outline the writer prepares, the producer will usually assign a director to the project. The **director** is responsible for the artistic elements which go into a television production.

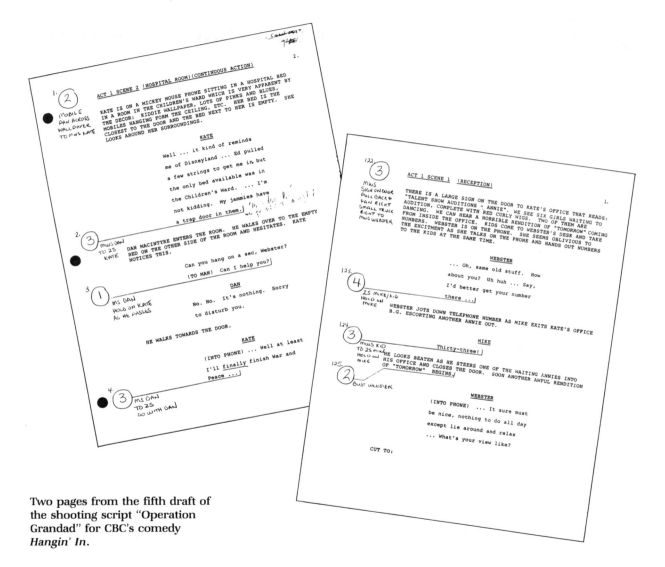

ACT 1 SCENE 2 (HOSPITAL ROOM) (CONTINUOUS ACTION)

② MOBILE PAN ACROSS WALLPAPER TO MWS KATE

KATE IS ON A MICKEY MOUSE PHONE SITTING IN A HOSPITAL BED IN A ROOM IN THE CHILDREN'S WARD WHICH IS VERY APPARENT BY THE DECOR: KIDDIE WALLPAPER, LOTS OF PINKS AND BLUES, MOBILES HANGING FORM THE CEILING, ETC. HER BED IS THE CLOSEST TO THE DOOR AND THE BED NEXT TO HER IS EMPTY. SHE LOOKS AROUND HER SURROUNDINGS.

KATE

Well ... it kind of reminds

me of Disneyland ... Ed pulled

a few strings to get me in but

the only bed available was in

the Children's Ward. ... I'm

not kidding. My jammies have

a trap door in them.

③ MWS DAN TO 2S KATE

DAN MACINTYRE ENTERS THE ROOM. HE WALKS OVER TO THE EMPTY BED ON THE OTHER SIDE OF THE ROOM AND HESITATES. KATE NOTICES THIS.

Can you hang on a sec, Webster?

(TO MAN) Can I help you?

③① MS DAN HOLD ON KATE AS HE PASSES

DAN

No. No. It's nothing. Sorry

to disturb you.

HE WALKS TOWARDS THE DOOR.

KATE

(INTO PHONE) ... Well at least

I'll finally finish War and

Peace ...

④③ MS DAN TO 2S GO WITH DAN

ACT 1 SCENE 1 (RECEPTION)

122 ③ MWS SIGN ON DOOR PULL BACK & PAN RIGHT SMALL TRUCK RIGHT TO MWS WEBSTER

THERE IS A LARGE SIGN ON THE DOOR TO KATE'S OFFICE THAT READS: "TALENT SHOW AUDITIONS - ANNIE". WE SEE SIX GIRLS WAITING TO AUDITION, COMPLETE WITH RED CURLY WIGS. TWO OF THEM ARE DANCING. WE CAN HEAR A HORRIBLE RENDITION OF "TOMORROW" COMING FROM INSIDE THE OFFICE. KIDS COME TO WEBSTER'S DESK AND TAKE NUMBERS. WEBSTER IS ON THE PHONE. SHE SEEMS OBLIVIOUS TO THE EXCITEMENT AS SHE TALKS ON THE PHONE AND HANDS OUT NUMBERS TO THE KIDS AT THE SAME TIME.

WEBSTER

... Oh, same old stuff. How

about you? Uh huh ... Say,

I'd better get your number

there ...

123 ④ 2S MIKE/KID HOLD ON MIKE

WEBSTER JOTS DOWN TELEPHONE NUMBER AS MIKE EXITS KATE'S OFFICE B.G. ESCORTING ANOTHER ANNIE OUT.

124 ③ MWS KID TO 2S MIKE HOLD ON MIKE

MIKE

Thirty-three!

HE LOOKS BEATEN AS HE STEERS ONE OF THE WAITING ANNIES INTO HIS OFFICE AND CLOSES THE DOOR. SOON ANOTHER AWFUL RENDITION OF "TOMORROW" BEGINS.

125 ② BUST WEBSTER

WEBSTER

(INTO PHONE) ... It sure must

be nice, nothing to do all day

except lie around and relax

... What's your view like?

CUT TO:

Two pages from the fifth draft of the shooting script "Operation Grandad" for CBC's comedy *Hangin' In*.

The director will work with the writer to produce a **master-scene-script**. The master-scene-script usually gives a complete account of all that happens in every scene, including the dialogue. In the preparation of the master-scene-script and in later stages of the production, the director will pay particular attention to the artistic aspects of the program.

When the master-scene-script is approved, a shooting script is produced. The **shooting script** typically includes most of the **technical details** needed for translating the written material in the master-scene-script into sound and picture images that can be captured on film or videotape. If both a master-scene-script and shooting script are used in a production, the shooting script often leaves out the dialogue, giving only the shots, camera angles and technical information needed by the director and **technical crew**.

While the script is being developed, the director casts performers for roles in the production. In some television productions, the director delegates this responsibility to a **casting director**. In the meantime, the director works with **lighting personnel, set designers, costuming** and **property departments** as well as **video** and **audio engineers** in planning the technical features of the program.

When performers are cast, rehearsal begins under the director's supervision. During rehearsal, the director will coordinate all of the technical elements with the performers' actions to develop a smoothly running production. In large productions, an assistant director helps the director to coordinate those aspects of the production for which the director is responsible.

When all parts of the production have been carefully combined, the program is ready for broadcast or, more commonly, for taping. On taped programs, editing permits the director to shoot scenes in an economical order. Scenes are seldom taped or filmed in the same order in which they are seen on television. All the scenes

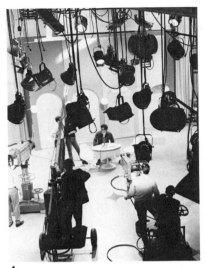

Elaborate lighting systems illuminate studio set.

The properties department provides "props" for television programs.

that take place in the same location will be shot at the same time. The shots are later put into the proper order by the film or tape editor working closely with the director.

Camera operators and engineers set up equipment to film the scenes in the way called for by the director in the shooting script. Lighting crews ready their equipment. Makeup people prepare the performers cosmetically for appearing before the cameras. Costume people insure that the proper clothing is worn by the cast, and property people make certain that the scene contains the appropriate props.

Unless the production is live, scenes which do not meet the standards of the director can be reshot, adjusting for the errors made in previous shots. Each segment that is shot is called a **take**. Some productions involving difficult scenes use dozens of takes to film one segment the way that the director wants it for the final production.

When all segments have been captured on tape, or film, the **editor** goes to work. The editor assembles the segments in the order called for by the script. This phase is called **post-production**.

Post-production involves other technical manipulations as well. Sound effects, additional applause and background music are usually added during this phase. Laughter may be added to the sound track. **Credits**, indicating individual contributions of personnel to the production, and titles are added during the post-production phase. When the edited material meets with the approval of the director and producer, the program is ready for broadcast.

Tell Me A Story

From the earliest times until the present, people have been captivated by stories. Young children climb into the laps of adults and plead with them to "tell me a story." Telling stories is the bread and butter of the television industry.

No matter how the stories are classified (western, adventure, mystery, comedy), their structure is basically the same. From the ancient Greeks to the most recent television blockbuster, stories have consisted of similar elements arranged in similar ways.

There are three essential parts to a television story — the beginning, middle and conclusion. It sometimes helps to think of them as acts in a play, but no matter what they are called, each part serves several special purposes.

Almost as soon as the program begins, the audience is introduced to the main characters in the story. This points to the importance of characters to a story. Although they are sometimes animated drawings of animals or even mechanized objects like robots, characters are an essential ingredient in the television story. Characters provide the action which moves the story along.

The first main character viewers usually see is the hero or

A conflict is developed in the first part of a television narrative, such as CBC's drama *Seeing Things*, starring Louis Del Grande as Louis Ciccone, a news reporter who has visions which involve him in dangerous situations and which help him to solve mysteries.

heroine, referred to as the **protagonist**. Some stories have two main characters. Often, the second character introduced is the villain, the **antagonist**.

Stories have villains for one main reason. It is the villain's job to conflict with the hero or heroine or to create a *problem* which the hero or heroine must solve.

Another ingredient is presented in the first act. This ingredient is the *negative consequence*. What this means is, if the hero or heroine fails to solve the problem, something terrible will happen to somebody or something! This creates the excitement which maintains the viewer's interest. The first act of a television story, then, combines four ingredients: hero or heroine, villain, problem and consequence.

During the second part of a television story, the writer makes the hero's or heroine's problem more complicated or intensifies the conflict between the hero or heroine and the villain. These techniques add interest. The writer wants the viewers to wonder how the problem will be solved or the conflict will end.

The writer hopes that the viewers will be on the edge of their seats by the time the third part of the story takes place. It is during the third part that the problem is solved or the conflict ended. In most television stories, the hero or heroine works things out by solving the problem or ending the conflict. In some stories, however, the problem or conflict gets the best of the hero or heroine.

The ingredients of television stories are well illustrated in the *Happy Days* episode called "Richie's Flip Side." In this episode, Richie, the hero, is working as a janitor in a local radio station. When the station's popular disc jockey quits because of a salary dispute with the station's owner, Richie is offered the disc jockey's job.

Although he is nervous at first, Richie soon becomes comfortable with the new job. In fact, Richie's interest and pleasure in

The challenges facing the hero or heroine are increased in the second part of a television narrative, as in this scene and the scene opposite from CBC's *Seeing Things*.

his new celebrity status as a disc jockey begins to interfere with his relations with family and friends. Richie is so entranced by his position that he has little time for his friends and shocks his family by changing his mind about attending college.

By the end of the first act, the viewer has been introduced to all of the main ingredients. The problem established in the first act is: Will success spoil Richie Cunningham?

In this story Richie is both hero and villain. Richie is in conflict with himself. The "good Richie," a loving and dutiful son and friendly companion, is on a collision course with the "bad Richie," the ambitious and self-important disc jockey. If the "bad Richie" is successful in dominating the "good Richie," Richie will lose his friends and disappoint his family.

Second acts usually add complications to the central problem, making the hero's or heroine's task more difficult than was first imagined. Act two of "Richie's Flip Side" follows this pattern. The radio station's owner decides that a broadcast from Arnold's Drive-In will boost the program's popularity. Richie and the station owner go to Arnold's to make the arrangements.

At the drive-in, Richie's conflict intensifies. His friends want Richie to take part in their normal routine, but Richie says he's too busy making arrangements for the broadcast. After the arrangements are made, Richie approaches his friends to explain the situation from his point of view.

Richie tells his friends that he has hit a fork in the road of life, explaining that he's got a chance to make it big as a disc jockey. He says that this means he won't have as much time for his friends as he once did, but that's the price he must pay for success. After Richie leaves his friends' table, Fonzie suggests that they "rake him over the coals until he cries 'wolf'."

That evening at Arnold's Drive-In, Richie is prepared for the live broadcast. A large crowd has gathered at Arnold's, including Richie's family. The broadcast begins and Richie tries to get the crowd to applaud and request songs. Richie does not know that Fonzie has signalled to the crowd not to take part in the broadcast. When the first song ends, only Richie's family applauds.

As Richie's program continues things get worse. The crowd doesn't respond and Richie becomes nervous. He eventually moves to the table where Potsie, Ralph and Fonzie are sitting. Richie tries to get them involved, but they ignore him. Richie becomes entangled in the microphone cord he is using. The cord almost seems to be choking him.

Finally Ralph and Potsie persuade Fonzie to ease up on Richie. In the few minutes before Richie's program is scheduled to leave the air, Fonzie requests a song and the crowd shows its approval for the show by applauding.

By the end of the second act, Richie resigns as the disc jockey. He tells the station's owner that it's no good having all those listeners, if nobody is talking to him. He tells his family about his decision and confesses that he feels like he is giving up something exciting in order to do what he thinks is right. As the second act ends, it is apparent that Richie is still torn between "doing right" and having a career as a disc jockey.

Third acts are devoted to solving the problem established in the first act. Sometimes the ending is an unhappy one, but more often it is happy.

On "Richie's Flip Side," the problem is happily resolved. Act three is set in Arnold's Drive-In. Richie is sitting in a booth alone. While Potsie is listening to a portable radio, he and Ralph walk to Richie's table and sit down.

Potsie tells Richie that now that he's not a disc jockey, he will have to go back to being average. Ralph explains that being average is like vanilla ice cream.

Richie doesn't seem to like the idea, but Ralph explains that there is nothing wrong with vanilla ice cream. He tells Richie that vanilla ice cream has been around a long time because people like vanilla ice cream. It becomes clear that Ralph and Potsie are telling Richie that they still like him. The last act ends with the whole group listening to Richie's replacement on Potsie's portable radio.

The sequence of events which make up the story is called the **plot**. The plot is what happens, including the action, conflict, and outcome of the story. The description of the three acts which make up "Richie's Flip Side" is an account of the story's plot.

Table 5.1: *Dramatic Structure of "Richie's Flip Side"*

ACT 1 — **Beginning**	
Introduce Hero	Richie Cunningham
Introduce Villain	"Richie the C," self-important disc jockey
Introduce Problem	Will success spoil Richie?
Introduce Negative Consequences	If Richie chooses to be a disc jockey, he'll lose his friends and disappoint his family.

ACT 2 — **Middle**	
Introduce Complications	Richie's friends decide to teach him a lesson.
	Richie quits as disc jockey, but is not completely convinced that he has made the correct decision.

ACT 3 — **Conclusion**	
Resolve Problem	Richie's friends let him know that he is still liked even though he is no longer a celebrity disc jockey.

```
                    HANGIN' IN

                "OPERATION GRANDAD"

                     CAST #15

ACT 1   SCENE 1   RECEPTION       DAY 1            MIKE         1
                                                  WEBSTER

        SCENE 2   HOSPITAL ROOM   DAY 1            KATE         2 -11
                                  CONT. ACTION     DAN
                                                   ED
                                                   NURSE
                                                   SONIA
                                                   ROGER

        SCENE 3   RECEPTION       DAY 1            WEBSTER      12-15
                                  CONT. ACTION     MIKE
                                                   LAST ANNIE
                                                   TINA

        SCENE 4   KATE'S OFFICE   DAY 1            TINA         16-18
                                  MINS. LATER      MIKE
                                                   GINA

        SCENE 5   HOSPITAL ROOM   DAY 1            KATE         19-25
                                  LATER THAT       DAN
                                  DAY              SONIA
                                                   ROGER

ACT 2   SCENE 1   HOSPITAL ROOM   DAY 2            ED           26-28
                                                  KATE
                                                   NURSE

        SCENE 2   RECEPTION       DAY 2            TINA         29-31
                                  CONT. ACTION     GINA
                                                   WEBSTER.

        SCENE 3   KITCHEN         DAY 2            WEBSTER      32-34
                                  CONT. ACTION     MIKE

        SCENE 4   RECEPTION       DAY 2            MIKE         35
                                  CONT. ACTION     TINA
                                                   GINA

        SCENE 5   KATE'S OFFICE   DAY 2            MIKE         36
                                  CONT. ACTION     TINA

        SCENE 6   HOSPITAL ROOM   DAY 2            DAN          37-41
                                  CONT. ACTION     ED
                                                   KATE
                                                   SONIA

        SCENE 7   KATE'S OFFICE   DAY 2            GINA         42-45
                                  CONT. ACTION     MIKE
                                                   TINA

        SCENE 8   RECEPTION       DAY 2            MAN          46
                                  CONT. ACTION     WEBSTER
                                                   GINA
                                                   TINA
                                                   MIKE
```

```
SCENE BREAKDOWN CONTD. - "OPERATION GRANDAD" ...................../2

ACT 2   SCENE 9   HOSPITAL ROOM   DAY 2            NURSE        47-54
                                  CONT. ACTION     KATE
                                                   DAN
                                                   SONIA
                                                   ROGER

TAG               HOSPITAL ROOM   DAY 3            WEBSTER      55
                                                  KATE
                                                   MIKE
                                                   TINA
                                                   GINA
                                                   DAN
                                                   SONIA
                                                   ED
                                                   NURSE
```

Outline of scenes for "Operation Grandad" from CBC's *Hangin' In*, written by Carol Commisso.

The underlying idea that the story communicates to the viewer is called the **theme**. The underlying theme in the *Happy Days* episode takes the form of a lesson or message to the viewer. The lesson is "Close, personal friendships and family relationships are more important than being a celebrity." In other television stories, the themes may be an explanation of people's behaviour or their problems.

● **Investigation 5.1:** *Predicting The Outcome Of A Television Program*

Method:

1. View the first fifteen minutes of a thirty-minute dramatic television program available on videotape.

2. At the halfway point, each class member should write a paragraph describing what he or she imagines will be the conclusion of the program.

3. In class, discuss the ways that students finished the plot. In the discussion, try to emphasize the elements which appeared during the first half of the program that influenced how the students concluded the program.

4. After the discussion, show the final fifteen minutes of the program. When the program is completed, try to describe the elements in the first half of the program that set the stage for the action in the second half of the program.

Skills Developed: 1.12, 1.13; 1.21; 3.4

Set designing is one of the early stages of developing a television program. CBC's Bob Lawson works on a scale model.

The success or failure of a story often rests on the viewer's attitude toward the main characters. It is around and through the characters that a story's action takes place. Characters who act and speak in a manner that matches the story's plot and theme help to hold the viewer's interest. When speech or action fails to make sense in terms of theme and plot, the viewer becomes confused.

The places where the story's action takes place contribute to the viewer's understanding of and appreciation for the story. Called the story's **settings**, the locations provide a platform on which the action can build.

■ Investigation 5.2: *Examining How Well Or How Poorly Television Develops Characters On Dramatic Programs*

Method:

1. Select a dramatic program for this investigation.

2. Using a characterization check list similar to Appendix V, identify the attributes which are typically shown by one of the main characters.

3. In a brief essay, attempt to answer the following questions:

a. Does the character display the full range of attributes you would expect of someone in that situation?

b. Do the attributes seem to centre around one aspect of the character's personality or behaviour? Which aspect of personality or behaviour seems most important?

Skills Developed: 1.13; 1.15; 1.22; 1.23; 1.26; 4.3

Varieties Of Television Drama

Over the years, television drama has used three basic formats. In the early days of television, the main format used was the **anthology drama**. This format is still used today, but it is used less frequently than it was during the 1950s.

The CBC's *For The Record* series is a recent example of anthology drama. Beginning in the 1974-75 season, the series consists of a set of programs in which none of the elements of drama — plot, theme, character or setting — is the same from program to program. In other words, each program is unique and unrelated to the others.

The series is made up of dramas on timely subjects which are often controversial. In recent years, the series has focused on unemployment, the gap between parents and children, wife battering, the closing of a large daily newspaper, racism, and similar issues. According to the series' producer, *For The Record* is designed to challenge and provoke as well as to entertain.

By the end of the 1950s anthology drama had given way to another format, **episodic drama**. This variety of drama is organized around a set of characters who appear regularly in show after show. The *Beachcombers*, *Three's Company*, *Hangin' In* and *Happy Days* are examples of episodic drama. The main characters on each of these shows confront and solve new problems each time the program airs.

On the *Beachcombers*, Nick, Relic, Molly, Jesse Jim, Sara and Corporal Norman appear in most episodes. The setting for the stories is usually a small community on the coast of British Columbia. The stories typically focus on problems which confront the main character, Nick Adonidas.

CBC's *Seeing Things* is an example of an episodic drama.

During the 1960s and 1970s, episodic drama was the main format used for entertainment programming. By the end of the 1970s, commercial television had adapted an old format, the **serial**, to its prime time period. A serial is a dramatic form where a regular set of characters confront problems which continue from program to program.

The early days of film and radio had shown that well-constructed serials would keep audiences coming back for more, week after week. During the 1930s and 1940s, the adventure serial or cliffhanger was a popular form of entertainment for movie-goers.

Each week audiences would be treated to stories where a villain had created a problem for a hero which the hero would have to solve in order to avoid disaster. Just as the suspense was at its highest point, the serial would end, forcing the audience to return the following week to find out whether the hero was going to be able to solve the problem.

Serial radio dramas were aimed mostly at women who listened during the day. These serial dramas became known as soap operas because the shows were often sponsored by manufacturers of soap. A familiar ending to a day's soap opera was a "teaser" about the next episode. At the end of the program an announcer would typically say, "Tune in tomorrow when we learn. . . ."

From the early days of television, serials were a popular form of entertainment during the daytime. *The Edge of Night*, for example, was on the air for more than twenty-five years before it

---

◼ **Investigation 5.3:** | *To Identify Patterns In The Scheduling Of Television Programs*

Method:

1. Examine a weekly listing of television programs.

2. Identify and classify programs in relation to the time period when they are shown and the day of the week they are shown.

3. Identify the demographic characteristics of the people who are likely to be among the audiences for each of the time periods. (In television, "demographics," refer to the age, sex, education and economic status of the viewing audience.)

4. In class discuss the following questions:

a. Does television programming attempt to shape or to react to viewer habits and routines?

b. Television programming should not be offered between midnight and 6:00 a.m. because it is the period which attracts the smallest number of television viewers.

Skills Developed: 1.23; 1.26; 2.6; 3.4

---

ended in 1985. Set in the fictional town of Monticello, *The Edge of Night* focused on the work of two lawyers.

The complex and continuing series featured plots involving murder, greed, mistaken identity and revenge. According to one observer, nearly one-third of all the murders on television before 1975 occurred on *The Edge of Night*!

By the late 1970s and early 1980s, television serials had become an important part of the evening television schedule. *Dallas* and *Hill Street Blues* are two examples of serials presented during television's prime time period between 6:00 p.m. and 12:00 p.m.

Dallas is a continuing story about the quest for power that focuses on the Ewing Family. Series regulars like J. R. Ewing, Miss Elly, Bobby, Pamela, Sue Ellen, Lucy and others seem to be constantly involved in plots in which someone is trying to gain power at the expense of someone else.

The last episode in *Dallas'* 1979-80 season ended with J.R. being shot. During its 1980-81 season, *Dallas* kept its audience returning week after week to find out "Who shot J.R.?" The 1980-81 season ended by posing a new cliff-hanging question, "Who is the body in the pool?"

Situation comedy has always been an important element in television entertainment. Comedy is usually less costly to produce than other dramatic forms. Westerns, mysteries, adventures and soap operas often depend on settings which cannot be reproduced easily within a television studio. Comedy relies much less on such settings. Being able to produce a show or an entire series within a studio makes production of comedy cheaper than most other dramatic forms.

Situation comedies have a lower "fatality" rate than other dramatizations. Comedies attract audiences more successfully than westerns, mysteries or adventures. The higher success ratio for comedies makes them popular with production companies seeking to limit their financial risks.

■ **Investigation 5.4:** *To Develop An Understanding Of The Forces Which Influence Programming Decisions*

Method: *When a television program succeeds in attracting a large audience, television producers often try to imitate the program's successful ingredients. Another way television programmers and producers try to capitalize on success is to create a spinoff. A spinoff is a "new" program starring characters who originally appeared in a successful program. An example of a spinoff program is* **Laverne and Shirley.** *Laverne and Shirley were characters who originally appeared on* **Happy Days.**

1. Examine a current listing of television programs. Group the programs into the following categories:
a. game shows
b. dramas
c. westerns
d. soap operas
e. mysteries/detective
f. situation comedies
g. news
h. children's shows
i. public affairs
j. religious programs

2. Examine the list of programs in a single category. Try to determine if there are similarities among them which indicate that imitation is occurring. Describe the features of a "winning formula" for that category of programs.

3. Write a paragraph stating your views about the following: *Television viewers suffer when television programmers and producers imitate successful programs.*

Skills Developed: **1.11; 1.12; 1.13; 1.22; 1.23; 1.26; 2.6; 3.2; 4.3; 4.4**

This is the set for CBC's acclaimed children's program *Fraggle Rock.*

The riskiness of television production is also lower for comedies because comedies seem to remain more timely than the other entertainment forms. *I Love Lucy*, the first television comedy series to be produced on film, is still broadcast on a regular basis in sections of North America after more than thirty years.

Another reason comedy is an important element of entertainment programming is drawing power. Placed properly in an evening's schedule of entertainment, comedies draw large audiences which tend to continue watching that station after the comedy has ended.

■ **Investigation 5.5:** *Examining The Characteristics Of Different Types Of Television Programs*

Method:

1. Divide the class into groups of four or five students. Select one program category (e.g., situation comedy) for analysis by the group. Each group should select a different program category, if possible.

2. During a one-week period, each student should view three programs in the category the group is studying. While viewing each program, record observations about the following aspects of the program: plot, theme, character, setting.

3. Study your findings and record any common ways in which the program category appears to present plot, theme, character and setting.

4. Report your findings to your group. After discussion among group members, prepare a report for the class describing the main techniques used in the program category your group studied.

5. Discuss in your class the differences and similarities between program categories with reference to plot, theme, character and setting.

6. In a 300-500 word essay, compare a program you studied with any other discussed in class, using plot, theme, character and setting as the basis for your comparison.

Skills Developed: **1.13; 1.15; 1.16; 1.22; 1.23; 1.26; 3.3; 4.3; 4.4; 4.5**

Test Yourself

A. *Identification:* Explain the meaning and/or significance of the following in your own words.

program concept	production budget
sequence outline	director
master-scene-script	shooting script
casting director	take
antagonist	protagonist
plot	theme
characterization	setting
anthology drama	episodic drama
serial	

B. *True and False:* Indicate with the letter T or the letter F whether you think the following statements are accurate or inaccurate. If any part of the statement is false or inaccurate, use the letter F.

1. Scenes for television programs are always shot in the same sequence as they appear in the finished product.

2. There are two basic ingredients in most television programs: the hero or heroine and the villain.

3. Conflicts or problems are always solved during a television program.

4. Episodic dramas feature the same characters over many shows.

5. Television develops a story in essentially the same way as do movies and plays.

6. Anthology dramas more frequently employ suspense than do episodic dramas.

7. Situation comedies rely more on setting than on character development.

8. Situation comedies generally run longer than other forms of entertainment programming.

C. *Multiple Choice:*   For each question, indicate the response you think best answers the question.

1. The first step in the development of a television program is the:
   - **a.** character outline.
   - **b.** budget allocation.
   - **c.** program concept.
   - **d.** hiring of a script writer.

2. Camera angles, shot selection and other technical information are detailed in the:
   - **a.** shooting script.
   - **b.** master-scene-script.
   - **c.** program concept.
   - **d.** director's manual.

3. The sequence of events that make up a story is called the:
   - **a.** plot.
   - **b.** characterization.
   - **c.** climax.
   - **d.** conflict or problem.

4. The underlying idea of a story is called the:
   - **a.** plot.
   - **b.** protagonist.
   - **c.** climax.
   - **d.** theme.

5. Which of the following is characteristic of an anthology drama?
   - **a.** Conflicts are often left unresolved.
   - **b.** Each episode is unrelated to other episodes.
   - **c.** A single character is followed through a series of conflicts over many programs.
   - **d.** A serious subject is treated in a light-hearted manner.

6. Which of the following is characteristic of a serial?
   - **a.** Plots are usually filled with violence and murder.
   - **b.** New characters are introduced in each episode.
   - **c.** One conflict is the focus of several shows.
   - **d.** The program ends with a problem that is resolved in the following program.

7. Which of the following is both the most likely to be filmed in a studio and is the most economical of television genres?
  a. anthology drama.
  c. news.
  b. episodic drama.
  d. situation comedy.

8. Comedies are usually less expensive to produce than other genre in television because:
  a. Comedians work for lower pay than dramatic performers.
  b. Situation comedies have relatively small casts.
  c. Situation comedies are filmed in only a few days.
  d. Comedies are usually shot entirely in a studio.

9. The problem faced by a character who fails to resolve a problem is called a:
  a. negative consequence.
  c. conflict.
  b. protagonist.
  d. villain.

D. *Activities For Further Investigation*

1. Most, but not all, television dramas end happily. Using specific examples from television programs you have viewed, analyze your reactions to those programs which have happy and unhappy endings. Do you prefer programs in which conflicts are resolved over those that leave things "up in the air"?

2. In an essay, discuss which of the following elements you believe is most vital to the success of a television program: (a) plot, (b) theme, (c) characterization, or (d) setting.

3. Television schedules include episodic dramas, anthology dramas, serials, and situation comedies. In an essay, explain which type of program you prefer. What elements of your favourite genre do you find most appealing?

Television And The News

6

As late as the seventeenth century, people gathered at coffee houses to learn the most recent news and gossip in their community. Before the development of the public school and the daily newspaper, people kept informed about their world as part of their social activity.

People who were unable to read listened to others who could. Neighbours exchanged stories about local events and speculated about the behaviour of community members. What the coffee house lacked in depth and breadth of coverage, it often made up for in colourfulness!

Like those of the people of the seventeenth century, the lives of most Canadians today focus on family, work and leisure. Nevertheless, when Canadians are asked to list their concerns, their lists often include issues and events which are not directly related to their day-to-day experiences. The issues include such global concerns as the arms race, and such national issues as Canadian unity.

Today, a large proportion of Canadians say that they most often use television to find out what is going on in the world. In the same way that the daily newspaper reduced the importance of the coffee house as a place of learning about the community, so television has reduced the use of the daily newspaper as a source of news.

Television is the medium most Canadians use to inform themselves about the world, and, according to those who use it, it is the most believable source of information. Whenever a single medium becomes the main source of information that people have about the world, that medium deserves close examination.

Television news is considered by many to be an extremely

Participation via television in freedom marches, in war, revolution, pollution, and other events is changing everything.

MARSHALL MCLUHAN

■ **Investigation 6.1:**	*To Determine Which Medium Of Mass Communication People Consider Most Believable*

Method:

1. Use a questionnaire similar to Appendix VI, "Media Believability," to determine which medium of mass communication people consider most believable.

2. Arrange to give the questionnaire to a large sample of students in your school, to parents and to teachers.

3. Analyze your results, comparing the responses made by the different groups (students, parents and teachers) in your sample. Did the groups respond differently or in the same way? Report your findings in your class, keeping in mind that your sample was not a random sample.

4. Discuss the following question with members of your class: *Why do people seem to consider some media more believable than others?*

Skills Developed: 1.22; 1.23; 1.25; 3.4; 4.2; 4.3; 4.6

influential source of information. In fact, people rely so heavily on television news that some analysts believe that it defines which issues are and which issues are not considered important.

The more exposure a person has to an issue, the more likely it is that the person will think the issue is important. Because of this, the selection of news and the way in which it is reported help to shape the viewer's responses to a wide range of social issues.

Television news has been accused of promoting two contradictory tendencies. On the one hand, critics suggest that television makes people feel powerless because it presents so many

. . . the images overwhelm our ability to make judgments or handle our government and our lives because we are so continuously aware of the disruption that's going on everywhere.

ALISTAIR COOKE, *U.S. News & World Report*

complex issues each day. These analysts argue that the large number of complicated issues overwhelms people and makes them feel that they cannot influence events.

On the other hand, critics have also accused television of artificially fostering social action. These analysts state that some people manipulate television news to achieve their purposes. Those who make this claim point to carefully timed news conferences and "made-for-TV" protests as evidence.

Like the coffee houses of the seventeenth century, television has both advantages and disadvantages as a source of news about the world. It is important to assess the way that television news is gathered and distributed to viewers, to consider what is and is not regarded as news, and to evaluate the strengths and weaknesses of television news coverage compared to other methods of presenting news.

How An Evening Newscast Is Prepared

In television especially there is a large element of prophesy in covering the news because the equipment we use is so cumbersome, heavy and so expensive that we almost have to decide what the news will be *now*.

TRINA McQUEEN, former Executive Producer of *The National*

The preparation of a television newscast is a complex and demanding task. Although the program often lasts less than twenty-five minutes, putting together a newscast begins many days before air time.

Planning and preparation are of great importance. Producers of television news programs must be able to coordinate people to respond to events around the world. They must be able to react quickly to unforseen events that change the news agenda. Because most newscasts are aired "live" there is no opportunity for deadline extensions or for editing out mistakes.

By the time the newsreader, the person seen on camera, arrives at the studio, the creation of the news has been underway for many hours. In fact, the first steps in making the evening news are taken more than a week earlier. Using **wire services** (news transmitted around the world by telegraphic devices), press releases, newspaper clippings and other sources, a file is made listing the events that may provide a focus for news coverage during the coming week.

Listings may include scheduled press conferences with politicians, sittings of Parliament and provincial legislatures, meetings of national and international organizations, and major sporting events. The CBC calls this listing the *week ahead*. The list is updated daily and revised. A second list, called the *day ahead*, is made up of items that will be the focus of activity during that particular day.

The day ahead grows to include many listings. Because there is only room for fifteen or twenty items in a single newscast, careful thought must be given to deciding which items are most newsworthy and deserving of assignment to a reporter and camera crew.

The job of deciding which items will be covered belongs to the **assignment editor**. From an extensive list of potential items, the assignment editor selects those to be covered and assigns a reporter and camera crew. Reporters may be assigned to an item a day or two before the item will be shown or on the same day it is to be shown. When the reporters are assigned depends on the importance of the item, the desired depth of coverage and the difficulty of getting the reporter and camera crew to the place where the action is occurring.

This photograph shows incoming film being listed on a board in early CBC newsroom.

Throughout the day, meetings are held of members of the executive news staff. Producers, directors and editors are informed about reporter assignments and the latest news agenda. Setting the news agenda is the responsibility of the **lineup editor**. Using information collected by the wire services and the listing of reporter assignments, the lineup editor plans the order in which news items will be presented on the evening newscast.

A lead item, typically the most important item of the day, must be selected. Whether the lead item is a national or international event will influence the ordering of the items that follow. Items which seem related to one another are often grouped together. National items are often grouped with other national items and international news items with other international items, and so on.

In addition to choosing the lead item and putting the others in a suitable order, the lineup editor must consider an item's importance before deciding how much time it deserves. Even important news items rarely run more than two minutes. Less important items will be given less than twenty seconds.

The average newscast covers from fifteen to twenty items. Placing these items within a twenty-minute newscast requires that even the longest and most important items will have to be told in a concise manner. Reporters and camera crews in the field quickly learn to operate in a style that fits television's fast pace.

When reporters and their film or tape return from the field to the studio, film/tape and copy editors take over. The **film/tape editor** cuts the material where necessary and the **copy editor** adjusts the reporter's narration. In fact, reporters in the field sometimes film several versions of the same narration. This gives the editors several choices from which to select the one that they think best suits the topic and the time available.

Copy editors are busy throughout the day preparing the script for the newscast. Information taken from wire services or other

The complexity of television news gathering is reflected in the production of CBC's *The Journal*.

sources is rewritten in a style appropriate for television. In addition to concerning themselves with style, copy editors must always be aware of the need to match scripts with the visual material to be used.

On most days, the agenda for the evening newscast is constantly changing. The lineup editor revises the order of material to accommodate late-breaking items. A significant item that breaks just before air time may result in a new lead item and the need to reorder all the other items in the newscast. Some pieces may even be dropped or shifted to other newscasts.

The final hours before air time are spent in re-checking the technical apparatus that plays such an important part in the production of the newscast. Items gathered in remote regions are transmitted by satellite and microwave systems to the studio. **Graphic materials** are prepared and scripts are typed. Newsreaders spend time reading the script and making small changes in wording to aid delivery.

Even as the newscast is being broadcast to viewers, the process of gathering news for coming shows continues. Wire services continue to send in items. Reporters and camera crews move on to their next assignments.

News gathering continues throughout the night under the supervision of the **night editor**. The night editor operates the news desk. When it is 4:00 in the morning in Toronto and most Ontarians are sleeping, it is nine o'clock in the morning in London, England, and noon in Saudi Arabia. The night editor collects wire service material, assigns reporters to cover important items developing during the night and receives reports from reporters in the field.

The business of gathering and distributing news is a twenty-four-hour-a-day, seven-days-a-week job. Many people are involved whose names and faces never appear on the television screen. Many decisions are made which determine the structure and content of the news as well as the viewers' reactions to the world in which they live.

What Is News?

If . . . the news is conceived of as entertainment, we react to it like an audience instead of an electorate; we chuckle instead of scream.

Life magazine

From time to time, news has been referred to as "recorded history." This reference is unfortunate and misleading because the job of the historian and the job of the reporter are very different.

The historian's job is to describe events, place them in their proper context and explain how one event is related to another. The historian requires substantial quantities of information, the time to analyze the information and an overview of the period during which the events occurred. Though, on the surface, news gathering and distribution may seem similar to the tasks of the historian, they are really very different.

News gathering has a number of characteristics which distinguish it from the historian's work. To be considered newsworthy,

Canadian television networks make extensive use of satellites to transmit news from distant spots to Canadian homes. Here CTV's *W5* reporter Dennis McIntosh *(left)* interviews presidential candidate José Napoléon Duarte *(right)* in El Salvador.

an incident must have been just recently revealed or disclosed. An event may have occurred sometime in the past, but its value as news depends upon its not having been known until now. In contrast, historians typically deal with occurrences which have often been well known to many people for a long period of time.

Recent disclosure of an event must generally also be coupled with the rapid distribution of information about the event for it to be regarded as newsworthy. In an age of advanced telecommunications technology, the rapid spread of information about an occurrence has become a characteristic of news.

In order to be regarded as newsworthy, an incident must be clearly connected to people's immediate concerns. The events with which the historian deals, may, after considerable thought and analysis, be regarded as having been very significant in peoples' lives in the past. News is thought to have an immediate impact.

For example, in the period immediately before the First World War, the rate of inflation in Europe was very high. If television had covered the incident during the period, news reporters would probably have concentrated on the rapid changes in prices. They might also have shown the difficulty people had handling the enormous quantities of money they needed to purchase simple items such as bread. The news media would not have had the perspective to realize that the unstable economy in Europe was one of a number of factors that would eventually lead to the outbreak of war.

To the news media, incidents are often isolated from one another. Historians, on the other hand, seek the connections among occurrences as a way of understanding how one event influences another.

Another important difference between the historian and the reporter is that historians know that the events they are studying have occurred. Historians already know much of the material that is the subject of the work they will perform. News people must anticipate events. They must either make an educated guess about when an incident will occur or react quickly to an incident that has just occurred.

Historians seek the truth. They want to know what really happened and why. They want to provide a comprehensive picture of all the details which combined to create some event so that its importance in peoples' lives will be well understood.

News people want to alert people to the occurrence of some new event. This event, after later analysis, may prove to be less or more important than was first thought. The major difficulty news people face that historians do not is that they have little time for analysis.

Historians do not have to meet the deadlines set for an evening newscast. They can take their time. Historians gather their information carefully, sift the information, and fill in gaps. When they are ready, historians put their interpretation of events before their audience. News people must put what they know before their audience without much opportunity for analysis, detailed gathering of background information or filling in of gaps.

What Is Television News?

The decisions about what qualifies as news in a news telecast is based on many factors. Economics, the quest for ratings, and the nature of television as a medium each influence what television regards as newsworthy.

Economics and the Quest for Ratings

News programming is profitable for national networks and local stations. The competition among networks and stations for audiences and the advertising revenue large audiences bring plays a major role in defining what is news.

Popular commercial TV is not likely to face life's facts when it wants to leave a viewer in a serene state of mind.

JACK GOULD, *The New York Times*

Because items about sex or violence capture larger audiences, these items are often featured in newscasts during the period when the size of an audience is being measured. News is often defined as what best sells advertising space. Independently owned television stations which rely on local news telecasts to raise revenue are most likely to present what viewers want to see rather than what viewers really need to know.

In the competition for ratings, television news editors often look to other news sources such as magazines, newspapers and wire services to define what is news. Similarly, competing television news operations provide news editors with ideas for stories and features. If one station or network runs a successful feature, it is likely that a competing station will use the same idea in its newscast.

Fads and fashion also often dictate what is news to news editors. At certain times, a single issue appears to dominate public attention and virtually every television news operation reports about that issue.

At various times in the past decade, stories about the environment, religious cults, the arms race and special interest groups have dominated television news features. As quickly as these items appear, they disappear, giving the viewer the false impression that a problem or issue has been solved. It is often the case that the problem continues, but television news has turned its attention to a more current interest.

The Nature of Television

The outstanding difference between television and other news sources is television's ability to deliver a visual image rapidly. The speed and visual qualities of television news have contributed to its popularity and perceived believability.

The picture is the key element in the telecast. Most items are accompanied by a film clip. Even when there are no public figures

Television news takes place where reporters are assigned. The centre figure is CBC's Knowlton Nash in Israel in 1967.

to interview or special events to film, the editor will construct a visual piece to enhance the item. An item on the economy may be narrated by a correspondent standing in front of the Parliament Buildings in Ottawa. A crime item may be filmed at the scene of the event or on the steps of the courthouse.

The emphasis of television news on visual images has led critics to charge that television news is more interested in "getting the picture" than "getting the story." Some analysts claim that when editors are faced with a choice of running an item with a film or one without a film, they will typically choose the filmed item, even when the other item is more important.

Television's visual qualities impose on television news a bias for action stories over non-action stories. A car accident or a fire captured on film may be given preference over an item about unemployment or the announcement of a change in government policy.

Stories dealing with the nation's foreign policy, the activities of national leaders and other well-known personalities, and economic news dominate news telecasts. Television's preference for these themes reflects the problems in putting together a news telecast.

Television news editors must be able to anticipate where a news item will take place. They cannot send a camera to a city street corner and hope that something interesting or important will occur on that corner.

In advance of each news telecast, editors assign reporters and camera crews to locations where events are likely to occur. Seats of government or places of continuing conflict are the most likely areas to produce a news item for the day. The requirement of getting reporters and cameras to the scene of the story makes predictable events more "newsworthy" than unpredictable events. News occurs where the camera crew and reporter are sent to cover a story!

Television's bias towards the activities of well-known people has led some critics of television news to charge that telecasts ignore the problems of unknown people, the poor and the powerless. The poor and powerless have a harder time putting their concerns before television news people. As a result, they have been unable to bring many of their concerns to public attention. Because television is predisposed toward picture stories with action, groups that have traditionally been denied access to news media have begun to gain attention by staging events for the television camera.

Peoples' preference for action stories inclines editors toward crime and violence. Studies indicate that those who watch the most television tend to believe that there is more violence in society than actually exists. People who are heavy viewers of television news feel less safe and secure than those who acquire their view of the world from other sources.

Newscasts more frequently report crimes committed by members of one ethnic group against members of another ethnic group than crimes among members of the same group. In fact, most violence occurs between members of the same ethnic group. Airplane crashes are usually considered newsworthy while automobile accidents usually are not. A viewer of television news could infer that air disasters occur more frequently and involve more people than automobile accidents when the reverse is true.

In the early 1970s, United States Vice-President Spiro Agnew received national attention when he charged that television news editors were "nabobs of negativism." Agnew and others have charged that television focuses on "bad news" and conveys to the viewer a distorted sense of reality.

A 1971 study contradicted the observation that television is primarily a "bearer of bad news." Analysis of forty-five news telecasts containing over 800 individual news stories found that two thirds of the stories could not be labelled "bad news." However,

The media cover the Colin Thatcher murder trial in Saskatoon in the fall of 1984. While being taken from jail to the courthouse, Mr. Thatcher was the focus of attention from more than 45 media members from across Canada who were covering the trial.

bad news features were most likely to be the first items in the newscast.

Television is more likely to report the unusual than the commonplace. In defining unusual events as more newsworthy than everyday occurrences, television news editors exaggerate the occurrence of some events and minimize the frequency and importance of others.

Is News Managed?

Among the many criticisms of television news is the charge that some news people intentionally attempt to influence viewer attitudes. According to these critics, the personal biases of station owners, editors and reporters prevent viewers from forming their own conclusions about issues on the basis of thoughtful consideration of a balanced presentation of the facts.

Any attempt to influence news content is called **news management**. News management, a practice which inevitably distorts and limits the information people receive, begins with news sources and news gathering organizations.

Within a television news operation there are a number of people who are able to make their personal biases felt. In the case of privately owned television stations, station managers and owners are in positions to influence the news. The power to hire, fire and promote reporters is one way in which the station's owner or manager can influence news style and content.

Reporters quickly learn the expectations of management and seek to avoid actions which run counter to station or network policy. The desire to advance, a natural regard for those in authority, and the enjoyment reporters get from their jobs all contribute to a reporter's desire to comply with management's expectations.

The pressure is so constant in television news that it is often difficult for line-up editors and producers to stand back and take a long view. A man with his finger in the dyke is the last one you'd ask for the overall flood position. And yet, in Canadian television, it is the men with their fingers in the dyke who determine what makes the newscast.

PETER TRUEMAN, newscaster and author, in *Smoke and Mirrors*

Station managers and owners have the final word in determining the general philosophy of a station and the treatment of specific items. They may personally involve themselves in writing and editing copy. Controversial items may be avoided at the management's discretion and other topics may be downplayed or declared off-limits.

While station owners and managers are individuals who possess varying likes and dislikes, in Canada they tend to be male, white, upper-middle class and urban. The way they wield their influence generally reflects the values common to that group.

Editors, too, are in a position to manage news. The assignment editor is the person who assigns reporters to cover specific beats or stories. In making reporter assignments, the assignment editor decides what is covered and what is not.

The film editor, responsible for choosing and cutting the film to match the script, is also a "news manager." The tape/film editor may be talented in working with tape/film, but may lack an understanding of news issues. Those parts of the film which he or she cuts may be significant or provide a substantially different viewpoint than those parts which are included in the news telecast.

The wire service editor, the person responsible for selecting newsworthy items from among the thousands of items that come across the wire each day, is in a position to manage news. The volume of stories and the constant pressure of deadlines creates the conditions for rapid, subjective judgements about what is and is not newsworthy.

News is also managed by the individuals and institutions that news media report about. Every day a television newsroom receives hundreds of press releases from politicians, governmental and private organizations and from individuals who want their stories told. Public figures hold press conferences to put their issues before television reporters. The press release and press conference are two techniques people use to give a favourable impression of who they are and what they do.

The day-to-day relationship between reporters and their sources of information is another factor which increases the possibility of news management. In television, news-gathering reporters are sometimes assigned to a "beat," a single area to cover such as city hall, the police courts or the legislature. Beat reporters establish close contacts with the newsmakers. This relationship enables the reporter to develop an understanding of the news source that would not be as evident to a casual observer.

In addition to gaining an understanding of the workings of the institution he or she is covering, the beat reporter establishes diverse and close contacts within the institution. This increases the reporter's access to newsworthy information. However, this very closeness may also prevent the reporter from fully exploring contacts. Long-term involvement in covering one beat may lead the reporter to develop an identification with the institution and people being covered. The reporter may find it difficult to report critically about "friends," fearing either a loss of their friendship or an abrupt end to the flow of information.

This situation poses a problem. On the one hand, to gain access to newsworthy information, the reporter must establish close contact with institutions and people highly placed within those institutions. On the other hand, the reporter's closeness may prevent reporting about the news the reporter has access to!

Recognizing the dangers of a reporter identifying too closely with the individuals and institutions the reporter must cover, editors often rotate beat reporters to new beats. Television news departments also employ general assignment reporters who don't find out what they are going to cover until the day of the assignment.

General assignment reporters are immune from the problems created by long-term association with one news beat. They are, however, at a disadvantage as news gatherers when compared with those reporters who have long-established contacts or a familiarity with the workings of the institution they cover.

The idea of news management creates a negative impression. Yet given the vast amounts of information that have to be sifted and selected by a great many people, it is impossible to avoid some degree of "news management." Viewers who recognize this fact will probe more deeply and examine more critically the issues presented by television news.

Budget night, Parliament Hill, Ottawa, June 1982. The foyer outside the House of Commons is crowded with media and politicians anxious to let the nation have their opinions following the tabling of the Liberal budget.

■ **Investigation 6.2:**	*To Identify The Decisions Made By Newsroom Personnel In Bringing A News Account To The Public's Attention*

Method:

1. Arrange to interview a news reporter or news editor about a local news account of importance in the community in which you live.

2. Prepare a set of questions that will help you to find out how the issue was selected for reporting and how it was arranged for presentation. You will need to inform yourself about the issue and use this chapter as background for preparing your questions.

Among the questions to consider are: How did newsroom personnel become aware of the issue or event? What other issues or events were considered for reporting and broadcast? What criteria did the news editor use in selecting this issue for broadcast as opposed to other issues under consideration?

3. After the interview has been conducted, class members should discuss what they have learned about news gathering and reporting at the local level. A question on which to focus is: *How well does the local television news cover issues and events of importance to our community?*

Skills Developed: **2.2; 2.4; 3.4; 3.5; 4.1; 4.2; 4.4**

Is Television News Objective?

Critics disagree about the influence of television news. Some charge that television news is always liberal, calling for fundamental social change. Others claim that television news is conservative. According to this viewpoint television news helps to maintain existing policies because it fails to probe deeply into major social problems. A third view is that television newscasters fail to provide thorough analysis and interpretation of the events they report. By "letting the facts speak for themselves" and not making value judgements, television news fails to fully inform the viewing public.

These contradictory criticisms cannot all be valid. Television news cannot be reform-minded, reactionary and value free all at the same time. Nevertheless, the various charges raise some important issues that deserve examination. One issue involves the appropriate relationship between objective and editorial commentary in television news.

In spite of some adjustments to fit the nature of an electronic, picture-oriented medium, television news is based on reporting practices that date back to the days when the print media dominated news. During the period when newspapers ruled the news world, several reporting styles evolved which contribute to present television news-gathering techniques.

For the most part, the earliest newspapers were blatantly and admittedly biased. Many were organs for political parties, preaching the party's philosophy and attacking the opposition. George Brown's *Toronto Globe* was such a paper in pre-Confederation Ontario. Brown was the leader of Ontario's Liberal Party and his newspaper vigorously defended Liberal policies.

Readers of nineteenth-century newspapers expected them to be biased. They simply avoided those that opposed their viewpoint and read those that supported their beliefs. Editors and reporters made no attempt to separate editorial comment from "hard news."

But the newspaper as a political organ was limited in its appeal. Its narrow bias served to restrict circulation. The publishers' search for a wider readership required a change in reporting methods. At the same time as publishers were trying to reach new readers, the development of wire services made large quantities of news material available for presentation.

> I'm not asking for government censorship or any other kind of censorship; I'm asking whether a form of censorship already exists when the news that forty million Americans receive each night is determined by a handful of men responsible only to their corporate employers and is filtered through a handful of commentators who admit to their own set of biases.
>
> SPIRO AGNEW, Vice President of the United States

Born in Hungary, Joseph Pulitzer came to the United States in 1864. After serving a year in the Union Army during the American Civil War, he became a journalist. Eventually he owned several newspapers. His papers were among the first to include illustrations, news stunts, crusades against corruption, and cartoons. The Pulitzer Prizes, awarded annually since 1917 for achievement in American journalism, letters and music, are paid from a fund left by Pulitzer to Columbia University.

Under these new influences, two reporting standards emerged which have survived to influence news publication today. The first was fathered by Adolph S. Ochs (1858-1935), publisher of *The New York Times* at the end of the nineteenth century.

Ochs' contribution was the objective tradition of reporting. He demanded that his reporters present an even-handed treatment of news without an editorial bias. According to Ochs and his followers, the purpose of the newspaper was to report, not to expose or inflame. At this time, newspapers began to provide separate and clearly identified sections of the paper for editorial and interpretive reporting.

Joseph Pulitzer (1847-1911) pioneered the second enduring news tradition. To Pulitzer the purpose of news was to expose wrongdoing in high places and to lead the cause of social reform.

Although both traditions of news publication have survived into the age of electronic journalism, a number of factors have resulted in the objective tradition becoming more commonplace in television news. The rapid acceptance of television in North America and its success in supplanting competing sources of news made television news people cautious about interpretation in news programs.

Television programmers felt that television had the potential to radically change society. This led to a self-imposed censorship. General entertainment programming reflected community standards of language and morality. Television news programming, too, adopted a middle-of-the-road approach to delivering news.

Outside influences also joined to direct television news toward an objective, balanced reporting style over a more judgemental style. All television in North America is subject to licencing and regulation. In Canada the regulating body is the Canadian Radio-television and Telecommunications Commission (CRTC). The Federal Communication Commission (FCC) serves the same function in the United States.

Both the CRTC and FCC require television operators to provide news and public affairs programming which serves the public interest. The performance of networks and stations is periodically reviewed against standards established by the CRTC. The cancelling of a licence is extremely rare. However, the presence of regulating bodies and the possibility of losing their licence encourages television news producers to maintain the standards set.

The economic importance of news programming to television must not be underestimated in encouraging television news to be objective. The reputation and ratings of a network news operation is important both in terms of revenue earned by the sale of commercial time and in the status of the network among its competitors.

Local television stations, both independent and network affiliates, often look to news as a major source of revenue. Objective reporting is considered necessary to attract large audiences to news programs. Biased, subjective reporting is thought to limit the audience to those viewers who share the editorial position of the station.

Television news shows a preference for facts over analysis. Analysis or commentary is the result of a careful examination of facts after they have been collected. To analyze well there must be time to consider the data that has been gathered before forming an opinion about the information. By withholding information until it has been analyzed, television news would give up the major advantage it has over competing news sources: speed.

How Television Compares With Other News Media

The rise of television as the major source of news has meant more than a simple substitution of one news source for another. Each news source has different strengths and weaknesses. People

---

■ Investigation 6.3:

To Determine The Extent To Which The Form Of Mass Communication Affects The Way News Is Presented

Method:

1. Each member of the class should select one of the major news media (television, newspapers, radio), insuring that all three media are represented among the members of the class.

2. Observe the treatment of the news on each of the media for a twenty-four hour period.

Analyze television with reference to the following:

a. subject of each news item
b. length of each story
c. national, international or local focus
d. position of the story in the telecast
e. the use narrative or film clips to explain the story
f. the use of background information
g. the amount of editorial commentary

Analyze radio news with reference to the following:

a. subject of each news item
b. length of each story
c. national, international or local focus
d. position of the story in the broadcast
e. emphasis given to sports and weather reports
f. use of taped interviews or reports
g. use of background information
h. the amount of editorial commentary

Analyze newspaper news stories with reference to the following:

a. subject of stories located on the front page
b. length of each story (translated into the amount of time it takes to read the story aloud)
c. national, international or local focus

d. use of photographs

e. use of background information

f. the amount of editorial content related to stories covered on the front page

3. To what extent does the nature of each news medium influence the way it treats the news?

4. What are the most obvious similarities and differences in the way news is presented by each medium?

5. Are the differences among the various news media greater than the differences found among sources within the same medium?

Skills Developed: **1.11; 1.15; 1.22; 1.23; 3.4; 4.5**

I once spent a week or so studying what happened in the spring of one year, 1926, that I had always looked back on nostalgically. I looked at what was happening all over Europe and the British Isles — anything that undoubtedly would have been featured in the evening news. It was a nightmare: famine in India, unemployment riots in Germany, Armenians starving, Britain paralyzed by a general strike, France fighting in Morocco, an army mutiny brewing in Spain.

You read about these things only if you wanted to. Now we see it all happen on television.

ALISTAIR COOKE, *U.S. News & World Report*

need different skills to understand the messages of various news media. Criteria for deciding what is and is not newsworthy vary widely with the type of media.

Compared with other news media, television's main advantage is its ability to report events related to peoples' immediate concerns almost as soon as the events have taken place. Only radio has this same ability. Newspapers and news magazines are more likely to report about issues that are not highly placed on the public's immediate agenda of concern. Indeed, newspapers and news magazines may even "introduce" issues that then become public concerns.

There are three reasons why television emphasizes events that have been recently disclosed and are at the forefront of peoples' concerns. Television does not devote enough space in its schedule to investigate issues in depth. It lacks an investigative tradition. And, it is oriented toward capturing large audiences and holding the audience's attention for its commercial messages.

The treatment of the content of the news also differs among

In the late 1970s and 1980s a few Canadian television programs were developed to cover news stories in greater depth. Each Sunday evening, CTV's *W5* team of investigative reporters — Helen Hutchinson, Bill Cunningham *(seated)*, Jim Reed *(left)* and Dennis McIntosh — report on issues that are relevant to Canadians. W5 stands for Who, What, Where, When and Why — the classic questions of journalism.

the news media. **Comprehensiveness** refers to the breadth and depth of reporting. Television suffers in comparison with competing media in both of these aspects. A half-hour newscast on television contains about as much information as one page of newspaper copy. For this reason, television critics have charged that television is merely a "headline service," providing a listing of the most important or sensational events of the day without providing either analysis or background.

Newspapers and magazines are more comprehensive than television news. They are able to provide more space to the treatment of each issue. Reporters have more time to develop background material, check information and analyze the issues.

The mass news media help people to interpret the causes and consequences of events by providing editorial and background reporting. Time limits and reporting traditions place television behind other media in providing both editorial and background reporting.

Television's emphasis on the visual and on the unique and sensational is reflected in its lack of **continuity** compared with other media. Television news is less likely than newspapers, news magazines or radio to stick with a story for a long time or to provide a follow-up on an "old" story.

The content of television news is the least varied of the major news media. The daily newspaper presents a broad range of news coverage including international, national, municipal and community news. Features cover both the powerful and the less powerful in society.

News magazines, like newspapers, have considerably more space to fill than television. They report about areas that are ignored by television. Television's coverage focuses on stories about powerful and famous people, the economy, international relations and spectacular events such as airplane crashes or natural disasters.

Different news media are attractive to different audiences. Each media makes different demands on and offers different opportunities to the consumer. Among the various media, television makes the fewest demands on the consumer. The spoken word is believed to be more easily understood than the printed word. People who are unable to read the words used in newspapers or news magazines are often able to understand them when they are spoken on television.

The spoken word and the visual image of television makes it easier for the viewer to absorb television's message. These factors make television almost universally accepted as a primary news source. Consumers do not have to work as hard at keeping up with the events presented on television as they do with the events presented in newspapers or magazines.

The visual elements of television also give viewers a sense of the reality of the events and people covered in the news. There is no doubt that the ability of television to take the viewer to the scene of news has contributed significantly to the public's knowledge of the world.

Another factor helping to make television Canada's major source of news is its accessibility. Television reaches into almost every Canadian home. Newspapers and news magazines have been much less successful in penetrating homes. One reason is that newspapers and magazines are more costly than television.

Television news has limitations which make it desirable for consumers to use other news sources to make up for television's shortcomings. With few exceptions, television news is mainly a headline service, providing little more than a brief description of current events. Background, analysis and editorial content are minimal compared to the daily newspaper and most news magazines.

Unlike readers of print news media, television viewers are usually unable to go back over stories to check for subtle meanings

CBC correspondent David Halton delivers a report for CBC News on the exodus of Arab refugees from Israeli-occupied Jordan, July 1967.

■ Investigation 6.4:   *Television News Coverage*

Method:
1.   Select a variety of television news programs for analysis. Be sure to choose programs from different time slots and from different types of stations.

2.   Using a form similar to Appendix VII, "News Analysis Guidesheet," as a guide, record the same information about each of the news programs.

3.   When you have collected your data, compare the data from different programs. Some questions to consider include:

a. What similarities and differences do news programs occurring on different stations during the same time period exhibit?

b. What similarities and differences do news programs occurring on the same station during different time periods exhibit?

c. Do weekend news programs exhibit the same or different patterns than those which are aired during the week?

4.   Discuss your findings with other class members. Speculate about the meaning of your results. Record your opinions.

5.   After your opinions have been recorded, invite a local television news producer to class to discuss your speculations and examine your data.

Skills Developed: 1.15; 1.22; 1.23; 1.26; 2.7; 3.4; 4.2; 4.3; 4.4

---

or inaccuracies. Television takes viewers rapidly from one story to the next. Readers of print are able to pace their reading to their own needs and interests.

No single news source possesses a monopoly on the desirable qualities of news. The informed news consumer understands the need to exploit the best qualities of each of the major news sources.

Test Yourself

A. *Identification:* Explain the meaning and/or significance of the following in your own words.

week ahead	day ahead
assignment editor	lineup editor
lead story	film/tape editor
copy editor	night editor
news management	press release
beat reporter	news source
general assignment reporter	objective reporting
editorial	CRTC
comprehensiveness	continuity

B. *True And False:* Indicate with the letter T or the letter F whether you think the following statements are accurate or inaccurate. If any part of the statement is false or inaccurate, use the letter F.

1. Television news helps to define what issues the public believes are important.

2. News stories are generally presented in order of their importance.

3. News reporters usually attempt to explain the relationship between events in the way that historians do.

4. Television is considered to be the most believable news medium largely because it provides visual images with a story.

5. Television newscasts reflect a bias for accounts with action over accounts with little or no action.

6. Television news coverage pays too much attention to unimportant people or groups in society.

7. The majority of television news accounts could be called "bad news" reports.

8. Television news sometimes highlights violence and action accounts to attract large viewing audiences.

9. Newspapers and other news media often look to television for ideas about what issues are newsworthy.

10. Beat reporters may develop friendships with sources. These friendships may hinder the flow of reliable and meaningful information.

11. The CRTC acts as a censor for Canadian television news.

12. Compared to other news media, television provides little investigative reporting.

13. Television is the best source of information about the news in your local community.

14. More people receive news via the daily newspaper than from television.

15. Individuals who get all of their information about current affairs from television will have a broad understanding of current issues.

C. *Multiple Choice:* For each question indicate the response you think best answers the question.

1. Analysts have criticized television news because:
   a. television news makes viewers feel responsible for all the bad news reported.
   b. television news makes people feel powerless.
   c. television presents an unrealistically "rosy" picture of the world.
   d. television news helps to redistribute power in society.

2. The week ahead:
   a. is a document that tries to predict the news for the following week.

b. is a file of clippings and press releases related to current and future stories.

c. is a list of important public meetings and events scheduled during the upcoming week.

d. contains a list of reporter assignments for the following week.

3. The decision about which issues and events will be reported on a newscast is made by:

a. the assignment editor.

b. the lineup editor.

c. the newsreader.

d. the entire news gathering staff.

4. Which of the following is an indication of the importance of a news account in a given day's telecast?

a. whether it is an international, national or local story

b. the amount of time spent covering the account

c. the number of pictures accompanying the account

d. the use of interviews to enhance the report

5. Which of the following illustrates a difference between news reporting and the writing of history?

a. News reporting is not as accurate as historical research.

b. News deals with the most recent occurrences whereas history deals with more distant events.

c. News reports are more analytical than written history.

d. Unlike news gatherers, historians are interested only in the most important events that take place.

6. The average half-hour television news program contains:

a. under ten news items.

b. from ten to fifteen news items.

c. from fifteen to twenty news items.

d. from twenty to twenty-five news items.

7. Beat reporters:
   a. do not spend enough time covering one event or institution to do a thorough reporting job.
   b. may develop friendships with sources that prevent objective and critical reporting.
   c. have the same relationships with sources as do general assignment reporters.
   d. are most likely to be victims of news management by editors and station managers.

8. Investigative reporting is largely absent from television news because:
   a. television news reporters lack the journalistic expertise of newspaper reporters.
   b. television reporters are more concerned with the quantity than the quality of news.
   c. television news is chiefly aimed at providing the news sooner than other media.
   d. advertisers exert influence on reporters to avoid investigating events too thoroughly.

D. *Activities For Further Investigation*

1. In an essay, compare and contrast the work of the historian and the news reporter.
2. Comment on the statement: "Television deserves its place as the most believable of all news sources."
3. Make the following statement the focus of a research paper: "Television *makes* rather than *reports* the news."
4. To what extent can it be stated that television distorts rather than reports the news?
5. In this chapter, various problems related to television news gathering and reporting are discussed. These include news management; the emphasis on violence; and the absence of

analysis, follow-up reports and in-depth reporting. Some of these practices may be related to the nature of television as an electronic medium. Others may be habits inherited from other news media or developed over the history of television. Choose any single problem discussed in the chapter and make it the subject of a research paper. Try to trace the development of the problem. Provide illustrations of the problem and suggest ways in which television may improve its performance in the area.

6. In an essay, evaluate the advantages and disadvantages of using beat and general assignment reporters to cover the news.

7. Assume that you are a member of a group that is concerned about a local corporation that is polluting the environment. You have been frustrated by your inability to communicate your concerns to the media and the public.

   In an essay, propose a way in which your group could "stage" an event to draw the attention of television news reporters to your cause. Conclude by commenting about whether you believe "staged" news is a serious problem for consumers of television news.

8. According to comment in this chapter, television news has been charged with a number of failings. It has been accused of being overly conservative, radical and non-committal. Based on your research and viewing experiences, write an essay in which you evaluate which of these observations is the most accurate. Indicate your reasons for reaching your conclusions and suggest which of these stances you think is most appropriate for television news.

9. If you were forced to rely on only one medium for all of your news, would you choose to rely on television, newspapers, radio, or news magazines? Your concern should be only with the medium's presentation of the news and not with other information it transmits.

In an essay, indicate which of these media you would choose to rely on. Explain the reasons for your selection and indicate any concerns you would have about being limited to the medium you have chosen.

10. Television news has changed dramatically since the early days of television. The first newscasts were fifteen minutes in length and were anchored by announcers rather than reporters. Investigate the evolution of television news from its beginning to the present. Evaluate the progress that television news programming has made.

11. In the 1980s television news expanded to include programs which devote an extended time to the coverage of one or two issues. The list includes such programs as CBC's *The Journal*, CTV's *W5*, ABC's *Nightline*, and Public Television's *McNeil-Lehrer Report*. Compare the coverage of news in these programs with traditional newscasts such as CBC's *The National* or the *CTV Evening News*. Consider differences and similarities in such elements as the amount of investigative reporting, use of visuals, presentation of differing viewpoints and presentation of analysis.

Television And Politics

A new form of "politics" is emerging, and in ways we haven't yet noticed. The living room has become a voting booth.

MARSHALL MCLUHAN

Whenever an election is called, television's role in the electoral process is bound to be a matter of discussion, controversy and criticism. Television is a relatively new ingredient in political affairs. Although it was present before 1960, it did not become an important factor in political affairs until the United States presidential campaign of that year.

In less than twenty-five years, people have come to rely on television more than any other medium of communication for becoming informed about politics. Many analysts believe that television's influence on politics has been mostly negative.

Critics of television maintain that it does a poor job of informing people about the way decisions are made and how power is distributed. They claim that television has been used to manipulate voters during elections. Television, they argue, influences people easily, and people are swayed more by the way television presents political issues than by *what* the issues mean. They also claim that politicians have been influenced by television to do what they think will be popular with the people, rather than what they consider is the right course to follow.

Some critics argue that television poses a threat to democratic government. They reason that governments are accountable to the people while television is not. Television, they suggest, stands between the people and their government.

Other analysts think that television's contribution to political affairs has been mostly positive. According to them, television has made our society more democratic. Today, people are more informed about politics and more familiar with their political leaders than in the past.

Television has also changed the way people look at political

This is how the United States presidential candidates appeared to television viewers during the second presidential debate in October 1960. The photograph is untouched and was made off a television screen in New York City. Senator John F. Kennedy, left, Democratic presidential candidate, answers questions while Vice President Richard Nixon, the Republican candidate, waits his turn.

issues. In the past, people seemed interested mainly in issues affecting their local communities. Today, television helps people see how issues affecting them also affect others in the nation and even the people of other nations.

The 1960 United States presidential election is often regarded as the first election in which television played a decisive part. It was also one of the closest contests in political history. Only one-tenth of one percent of the popular vote separated the winner, John F. Kennedy, from the loser, Richard M. Nixon.

Many analysts claimed that the televised debates between the candidates determined the outcome of the election. Television enabled the lesser-known candidate, Kennedy, to defeat the better-known Vice-President Nixon.

People who *saw* the debates between Nixon and Kennedy on television said that Kennedy was the "more attractive" of the two candidates. People who *heard* the debates on radio said that Nixon was the "more effective" debater.

Television viewers said that they were impressed by the differences in *style* and *image* between the two candidates. Kennedy seemed cool, confident and youthful. Nixon, on the other hand, perspired and did not appear to have shaved well. Some analysts insisted that viewers were influenced more by the candidates' *looks* than by their grasp of the *issues*. The Kennedy victory was seen by these analysts as a victory for television's influence.

Eight years later, Nixon ran successfully for the presidency of the United States. The 1968 campaign became the topic of the book *The Selling of the President* by Joe McGinnis. McGinnis claimed that Nixon had been sold to the American people in the same way that advertisers sell laundry detergent. According to McGinnis, Nixon's media advisers manipulated voters with their use of television.

In 1968, Pierre Trudeau became leader of the Liberal Party and Canada's Prime Minister. Soon after, Trudeau called a national election. Trudeau's popularity with Canadians came to be known as "Trudeaumania." Some analysts claim that, like Nixon's campaign, the 1968 Canadian election campaign, particularly as it was covered by television, focused on the candidates' *styles* and not on their views about national *issues*.

By 1968, many analysts were growing alarmed about television's influence on politics. They suggested that, with television, to be elected required a positive television personality. *Style* was replacing *ability* as a requirement for political office. In the age of television campaigns guided by media experts, such analysts argued, awkward and uncharismatic people such as William Lyon Mackenzie King and Abraham Lincoln would not be elected.

News Coverage Of Elections

Television has replaced the newspaper as the most widely used source of information about politics. According to opinion surveys, people feel that television is the most reliable, informative, and balanced source of political news.

Research about television news coverage of politics has focused on two areas. One is the examination of how well television informs viewers about political issues. The second is the examination of the impact that television news has on the behaviour of voters.

Studies indicate two things: (1) People's trust in television news as a source of political information is misplaced; and (2) the influence of television on viewer attitudes has been exaggerated.

Thomas F. Patterson and Robert D. McClure interviewed voters before, during and after the 1972 United States presidential campaign. They wanted to discover in what ways people's opinions about the candidates and their knowledge of the issues were influenced by the way different media covered the campaign. In their study they considered many of the factors influencing people's views and voting behaviour. They placed particular emphasis on isolating and measuring the influence of television. A recent study of the 1980 Quebec referendum campaign confirmed many of the same results as the Patterson and McClure study.

According to Patterson and McClure, news coverage should help people become familiar with the issues raised during an election campaign. News coverage should also help voters judge whether candidates have the necessary qualities for public service. Indeed, according to Patterson and McClure, the qualifications of the candidates is the most important issue facing voters

CBC staffers cover the 1968 federal election.

in an election. A candidate's suitability for office should therefore be the primary focus of the media's election coverage.

Patterson and McClure found that television failed to meet these responsibilities. The results of their study, published under the title *The Unseeing Eye*, showed that television news coverage of political campaigns focused more on *style* than on *issues*.

Their study revealed that approximately 60% of television news coverage showed candidates in large crowds — shaking hands with voters, attending rallies and driving in motorcades. Less than 10% of the coverage showed or discussed the candidates on their own. Only 3% of the total news time was devoted to covering the issues involved in the campaign.

Political coverage on television news also failed to address the qualifications of the candidates. Only one percent of the total news coverage was devoted to the candidates' qualifications for office. When the question of qualifications was addressed, the usual form was to present the comments of one candidate about the qualifications of the others. Television news almost completely avoided its own analysis of the leadership qualities of candidates.

Television has been accused of contributing to the politics of *image* rather than issues. Image politics pay more attention to how politicians look and sound than to what they say. Some people are disturbed by image politics because they believe it deceives voters.

Studies such as *The Unseeing Eye* do confirm that television news dwells on images rather than issues. However, studies also consistently show that these images fail to influence voters.

Television news coverage of political campaigns does not add to viewers' knowledge of issues. The Patterson and McClure study found that those who relied on television as their major source of information did not increase their knowledge or understanding of election issues during the campaign. Voters who relied on

---

● **Investigation 7.1:** *To Compare Newspaper And Television Coverage Of An Election*

Method: 1.   Divide the class into two groups. Group one should rely totally on the newspaper during an election campaign. Group two should rely totally on television for campaign coverage.

2.   Each student should keep a record of findings and observations made during the campaign about the following:

a. What are the major issues in the campaign?

b. What are the positions of the major candidates on the major issues?

c. Briefly outline the qualities possessed by each candidate.

3.   Compare and contrast the findings of each group. Did one group succeed more than the other in identifying issues, candidate positions about issues, and qualifications of candidates for public office?

4.   Prepare a written or oral report about the value of television and of newspapers in informing the public about political issues.

Skills Developed: **1.22; 1.23; 1.24; 3.1; 3.5; 4.3; 4.4**

---

newspapers, on the other hand, did improve their knowledge and understanding of the issues.

Television viewers were unlikely to change their choice of candidates on the basis of what they saw. They simply did not gain enough new information to change their previous opinions about the candidates or the political parties. Newspaper readers were more likely to be influenced by the additional amounts of information they gained.

The amount of television news that people watched during

political campaigns did not have any bearing on their understanding of the issues either. Because television virtually ignored issues in favour of imagery, no benefit nor harm was provided for viewers who watched more or less than average amounts of television news. There was, however, a significant advantage for people who were frequent newspaper readers. They were found to have gained twice as much knowledge about election issues as people who seldom read newspapers.

In politics, people seem to be persuaded by information rather than imagery. According to Patterson and McClure's research, television news fails to provide enough useful information to voters during election campaigns to lead them to change their original views.

Political Advertising On Television

Television has changed the relationship between politicians and the people they serve. Before television, politicians communicated with people as they travelled through their political territories giving speeches and meeting the voters. Reporters covered political beats and wrote about elected officials and candidates for public office. Columnists assessed the politicians and the issues, offering their views to newspaper readers.

Television altered both the form and the content of the communication between politicians and the public. Vast audiences, made up of both interested and disinterested people, are now exposed to political messages sandwiched between popular entertainment programs. The importance of the reporter as an interpreter of the politician's message has been reduced. Even during those times when a commentary is provided, the politician's appearance seems to carry more weight than a reporter's interpretation of the politician's message.

■ Investigation 7.2: *To Determine The Extent Of Political Advertising On Television During National, Provincial And Municipal Elections*

Method:

1. Beginning at the call of a national or provincial election or two months prior to a municipal election, arrange with a group of students to sample systematically the political advertising broadcast on television during prime time.

2. Using a form similar to Appendix VIII, "Political Advertising on Television," keep a record of the length of the political advertisements being aired, the party or candidate being presented, the times of showing, and the type of advertisements used (issue or image).

3. Prepare your data for presentation to the entire class. Arrange your data on a bar graph showing the total amount of political advertising (in seconds) for each of the days in your sample. Begin with the date of the election call and continue up to the day of the election.

   Prepare another bar graph showing the amount of political advertising (in seconds) for the different time periods covered in your investigation (6:00 p.m. to 7:00 p.m., 7:00 p.m. to 8:00 p.m.; etc.).

4. What patterns do you observe in your data? Is the amount of political advertising the same throughout the campaign or are there some periods during which there is more advertising? How are political advertisements spread out across the evening's viewing schedule? Does the frequency and nature of political advertising change during the course of the campaign?

Skills Developed: **2.3; 3.1; 4.1; 4.2; 4.3; 4.4; 4.6**

The use of television by politicians to communicate with the electorate is most noticeable during election campaigns. Television stations carry political advertisements endorsing some candidates and condemning others. The advertisements range from fifteen-second to thirty-minute messages.

The value placed on television advertising can be measured in part by examining the candidates' political organizations. Media consultants are among the best paid campaign workers. Producing political advertisements and purchasing television time are often major campaign costs. Some analysts point to the amount of money and personnel devoted to television advertising as evidence of television's influence during elections.

The use of television during campaigns has raised concern that television undermines traditional democratic values and electoral practices. Again, the most common criticism is that political advertising is image rather than issue oriented.

Political advertising on television is accused of appealing to the voters' emotions rather than to their intelligence. Critics suggest that political advertising treats politicians like any other product that is advertised on television. Viewers are encouraged to select political candidates in the same manner as they choose among competing brands of toothpaste.

Studies reveal that popular beliefs about the nature and effect of political advertising, like popular beliefs about the effect of television news coverage of election campaigns, are inaccurate. Patterson and McClure in their study identified two types of political advertisements. Each had a markedly different impact on viewers.

Image Advertising

The political advertisement that gets the most attention from critics is the **image advertisement**. It is usually brief and de-

Mulroney, Turner and Broadbent debate on television, summer 1984. The impact of television has led political leaders to concern themselves with their television image.

signed to create the impression that the candidate is a good person.

According to Patterson and McClure, the image advertisement tries to present the candidate as articulate, courageous and attractive. Image advertising often ignores the candidate's policies or actual personal qualities. The purpose is to make the candidate match the viewers' picture of an ideal candidate.

The popular notion is that viewers are convinced by the images presented in such advertisements. Critics claim that voters become emotionally attached to an image that has been created by half-truths.

Research, however, indicates that image advertisements have little impact on the viewer. Voting polls taken before, during and after people had been exposed to advertising campaigns reveal that such advertisements did not lead viewers to change their views or their votes.

When people watch political advertisements, they do so with pre-existing views and biases. These values seem to be the most important factors in determining their responses to image advertisements. The general tendency is for people to respond positively to images, ideas and personalities that are consistent with or similar to their own values. On the other hand, people reject images, ideas and personalities with which they disagree.

In the 1972 study by Patterson and McClure, Nixon supporters reacted favourably to advertisements which praised Nixon. They were negative toward advertisements for George McGovern, Nixon's opponent. Nixon supporters found McGovern advertisements unbelievable. McGovern supporters liked what they saw in McGovern advertisements and reacted negatively to advertisements for Nixon.

Other factors are more important than image advertising in shaping the way people vote. Educational level, gender, ethnic background and income level contribute to people's political perspectives. Image advertising is not powerful enough or long-lived enough to overcome these influences.

Issue Advertising

The second type of political advertisement is the **issue advertisement**. The issue advertisement differs from the image advertisement in a number of ways. Issue advertisements address issues and policies in the campaign. The focus of issue advertising is on what the candidate believes or intends to do rather than how the candidate looks.

Issue advertisements are different from image advertisements in appearance as well as content. Image advertisements emphasize the visual. They look like commercials promoting consumer products. Issue advertisements, on the other hand, emphasize the candidate's ideas. They frequently show the candidate speaking directly to the voter. In some, the candidate's or the party's name is shown on the screen and a narrator's voice delivers the political statement. In all issue advertisements, the visual element is downplayed so that it will not detract from the simple and straightforward message.

Issue advertisements tend to be longer than image advertisements. They are longer because it takes more time to make a statement for the voter to consider than it does to create a visual impression.

Issue advertisements present one candidate's views positively and the other candidates' views negatively. Viewers expect this bias. During an election campaign they see advertisements for all major political parties and almost all candidates. Under such circumstances, it is unlikely that viewers will be "brainwashed" by repeated exposure to a single point of view.

Issue advertisements provide a useful function during a political campaign. They help to educate voters about the key issues in the campaign and inform them about the candidates' positions on the issues.

Patterson and McClure's study reveals that, when television viewers are exposed to issue advertisements, they increase their knowledge about election issues. It is interesting to note that viewers of television news displayed no corresponding increase in knowledge. In other words, televised issue advertising was a better source of voter information than television news!

Some of the major concerns about television's impact on the political process appear to be unfounded. Voters see what they want to see rather than what advertisers want them to see. People take politics too seriously to change their votes without good reason. In short, voters are too smart to be manipulated by television.

Televising The House Of Commons And Provincial Legislatures

In August of 1953, United States President Dwight D. Eisenhower addressed the Canadian Parliament. The event was televised, marking the first entry by television into the House of Commons. Television coverage of the federal government's proceedings evolved slowly over the two decades that followed.

For a long time, television's attempt to show how the federal government conducts business was limited to ceremonial events such as the opening of Parliament, the Speech from the Throne and Royal visits. The CBC made a suggestion to film everyday parliamentary proceedings in 1967.

The first approved entry of television to cover everyday government business occurred on January 14, 1970. The CBC covered the House of Commons' External Affairs Committee meeting to discuss Canadian aid to Nigeria. In June of 1975, television cameras were admitted experimentally to the proceeding of a Senate Committee discussing a bill about marijuana. An excerpt was later shown on a newscast.

While the federal Parliament was slowly breaking down the barriers that kept television on the outside, a number of provincial legislatures moved more quickly. In March 1971, Nova Scotia became the first Canadian province to allow television coverage of some of its legislative proceedings.

In March 1972, Alberta became the first province to adopt full-time coverage of its legislature. Ontario gave television access to its legislature on an experimental basis in 1976. The federal government caught up to these provinces on October 17, 1977, when it began full-time television coverage of the House of Commons.

Provincial legislatures and the federal government were cautious about giving television access to their activities for a number

Television cameras record a Senate legal affairs committee hearing in 1975, the first time television cameras (or still cameras) were allowed to film a parliamentary committee in session.

of reasons. There was widespread concern that television would be a disruptive influence rather than a constructive presence in the legislature. A few in government were not anxious to let the public see the public's business being conducted because they feared that such exposure would make politicians more accountable.

Many of those who opposed televised coverage of government argued that politicians would play to the cameras rather than conduct business as usual. It was feared that a new model for a politician would be created, valuing style and appearance and minimizing other qualities.

Some politicians wished to protect the public from seeing the government conducted in a style that was less dignified than the public suspected. As those who watch televised proceedings of Parliament and the provincial legislatures know, it is common for members to shout at and heckle opposing politicians. Calls for order by the Speaker of the House are frequent. It was feared that exposing parliamentary style to the Canadian people would bring discredit to all politicians and to the institution of Parliament and the provincial legislatures.

Before allowing television into parliamentary chambers, politicians wanted to protect themselves from the critical eye of the camera. As a result, when television was finally admitted to legislatures, restrictions were placed on how cameras could be used.

For example, it was feared that the public, many of whom do not realize how much government business is carried on in committees and not in the legislature itself, would react badly to the fact that many sessions of the legislatures are poorly attended. Hence, in Parliament the cameras are permitted to focus only on the person speaking. Panning the chamber is not permitted. Since members of one's party typically gather around the person speaking, when the cameras are focused on the member who is speaking, viewers do not see the empty seats in the chamber.

■ Investigation 7.3:

To Evaluate Television Coverage Of Parliament Or Your Provincial Legislature

Method:

1. When you have obtained the necessary written permission, videotape a session of Parliament or your provincial legislature and play it for the class.

2. After viewing, discuss the following questions:

a. Do speakers appear to be "playing to the cameras"?

b. Does television's presence appear to affect the legislative process in any way?

c. Does the presence of television bring credit or discredit to the proceedings or to the institution of Parliament or your provincial legislature?

d. Are the restrictions on camera movement necessary?

e. Are you surprised that few people watch the televised proceedings of Parliament and their provincial legislatures? Why or why not?

f. Do you think that televising Parliament and the provincial legislature is worth the time and money spent? Why or why not?

g. What impact has televising government proceedings had on the Canadian political system?

Skills Developed: **1.22; 1.23; 1.25**

Many of the fears that delayed the coming of television to governmental proceedings have proved to be unfounded. Restrictions on camera use have kept the camera a neutral presence. Viewing audiences have generally been small and there have been no strong reactions to the televised proceedings of government.

The real or imagined drawbacks which were supposed to have accompanied television into the chambers of government have been offset by the public's increased ability to see the actions of its representatives.

The Regulation Of Political Broadcasting

Television time for advertising, particularly on a national level, is extremely costly. The cost keeps all but the wealthiest enterprises from addressing a national audience. The Broadcasting Act and the Canada Elections Act provide regulations to insure a fair distribution of network time among the major political parties.

The Canada Elections Act requires that each Canadian network and private station set aside six and one-half hours of broadcast time for political broadcasts in the four weeks preceding an election. The time provided must be prime time. This rule keeps the networks and private stations from slotting political broadcasts during periods when few viewers would see them.

In accordance with the Elections Act, representatives of the major political parties meet to negotiate how the six and one-half hours will be shared among the parties. As a general rule, the distribution of time is based on the results of the last election. The party that won the election receives the greatest portion of time. The other parties receive shares proportional to their success in the last election. No specific guidelines, however, govern the negotiations other than that the distribution should be fair. If the parties fail to reach agreement, the CRTC acts as an umpire.

Once agreement has been reached about the sharing of time, the parties enter into negotiations with the networks and private stations about the actual allocation of time within the program schedule. Stations offer both commercial and program time. Commercial time is used for brief spots ranging from fifteen seconds to a minute. Program time is used for longer political broadcasts which may last from five minutes to half an hour.

Television camera crews prepare their equipment in the corridors of the House of Commons in anticipation of a vote against the government which could lead to the defeat of the Clark administration, 1979.

The programming day on network television is composed of time belonging to the networks and time belonging to the local network affiliates. Networks and affiliates meet to discuss what portion of the time granted to political broadcasting will come from the network's time and what from the affiliate's time.

The Elections Act forbids all stations to provide more time to one party or candidate, above the six and one-half hours provided by law, without making the same amount of time available to all other parties. Networks and affiliates and private stations are not allowed to offer special advertising rates to one party and not to the others.

These restrictions are intended to keep stations from showing favouritism to one party by giving it better treatment. Violations of these and other regulations of the Elections Act are punishable by both fines and suspension of the broadcaster's licence.

The six and one half hours that television stations must provide for political broadcasting is paid for by the parties at rates established by the stations. In addition to this paid time, the Elections Act requires that stations provide free air time for political broadcasts. The amount of free time provided is negotiated between the stations and the parties. The distribution of time is based on the same formula used to distribute paid time.

The regulations of the Canada Elections Act are designed to give the major political parties equal opportunities to get their messages to the voters and to prevent television stations from using their control of air time to influence election outcomes. These regulations are motivated by the desire to protect the public from manipulation by political broadcasts.

Dramatization in political broadcasts is prohibited. Each political message must be followed by a statement identifying the sponsor of the message. This requirement enables the viewer to better detect bias in the message and to know which groups support the various parties or candidates.

Political broadcasts on television are also restricted to a period beginning twenty-nine days before and ending two days before election day. The ban on advertising in the forty-eight hours before election day is designed to allow voters to make their decisions free of last-minute influence.

The regulations affecting political broadcasing in Canada are relatively few. This is remarkable in view of the importance and complexity of both the mass media and democratic government. The regulations are generally approved of by all political parties.

One criticism of the regulations, however, is that they give an advantage to established parties over newer or less popular parties. Because the allocation of air time is based on a party's success in the previous election, established parties receive the greatest share of time available. Smaller parties are denied access to the air time they need to help build a following. For the most part, however, Canada's regulations for political broadcasts seem to balance the rights of citizens to be informed without bias with the rights of the political parties to get their messages to voters.

Test Yourself

A. *Identification:*   Explain the meaning and/or significance of the following in your own words.

image advertisement	issue advertisement
manipulation	Canada Elections Act
equal time	

B. *True And False:*   Indicate with the letter T or the letter F whether you think the following statements are accurate or inaccurate. If any part 'of the statement is false or inaccurate, use the letter F.

1. Television is the major source of information about politics for most Canadians.
2. People are wise to place their trust in television's reporting about politics.
3. Voters are easily influenced by image advertisements.
4. About half of all news coverage of elections focuses on campaign issues.
5. Television coverage of politics seldom leads voters to change their attitudes about candidates.
6. People's knowledge about politics will increase if they watch more television.
7. Image advertisements appeal to voter's emotions.
8. There is little danger that voters will be brainwashed by repeated exposure to image advertisements during election campaigns.
9. Issue advertisements contribute significantly to the viewer's understanding of campaign issues.
10. Each major political party receives an equal share of the six and one-half hours of broadcast time provided by the Broadcasting Act during an election campaign.

C. *Multiple Choice:* For each question indicate which response you think best answers the question.

1. When did television's possible influence on politics first come to public attention?
   a. 1950
   b. 1960
   c. 1970
   d. 1980

2. Which of the following attributes of a candidate should be addressed by television news coverage during a campaign?
   a. speaking ability

    b. ease with large crowds

    c. campaign style

    d. suitability for elected office

3. Television most frequently focuses on a candidate's
   a. style.
   b. background.
   c. position on issues.
   d. suitability for elected office.

4. People who get most of their information about elections from television:
   a. do not greatly increase their understanding of the issues.
   b. gain substantially in their awareness of election issues.
   c. are able to identify differences among candidates better than those who do not watch television.
   d. are less interested in politics than people who get most of their election information from newspapers.

5. Which of the following are characteristic of image advertisements?
   a. They are more than one minute long.
   b. They address important election issues.
   c. They depict the candidate as someone who possesses ideal qualities.
   d. They show the candidate speaking directly towards the camera.

6. People who view political advertisements on television:
   a. often find the advertisements confusing.
   b. do not know enough about the issues to decide what they should think.
   c. tend to agree with whatever they hear at the time.
   d. accept only those ideas that are similar to the ideas they already believe.

7. Image advertisements are ineffective because:
   a. people find them unbelievable.
   b. people place too much importance on elections to be swayed by so little information.
   c. people seldom change their political beliefs or preferences for candidates.
   d. most voters basically distrust politicians.

8. The first televised session of Canada's Parliament took place in:
   a. 1947   c. 1961
   b. 1953   d. 1970

9. The first province to introduce full-time coverage of its legislature was:
   a. Quebec.   c. Alberta.
   b. Ontario.   d. Nova Scotia.

10. Some people have been critical of regulations affecting political broadcasts in Canada because.
    a. the cost of purchasing television time is too great.
    b. regulations increase the likelihood that voters will be manipulated by advertisements.
    c. regulation of political broadcasts is unacceptable in a democratic society.
    d. larger parties have advantages over small political parties.

D. *Activities For Further Investigation*

1. Based on your reading of this chapter and other research, comment on the following statement: "Television has contributed more than it has detracted from democracy."

2. Select any local or national political figure with whom you are familiar. Write a paragraph in which you describe your

feelings about the individual. Evaluate to what extent your attitudes have been shaped by the politician's style and to what extent it is based on your reaction to the politician's position on issues.

3. Do you think the presence of television cameras in Parliament and in provincial legislatures has been a valuable addition to Canadian democracy? In an essay, outline the benefits and hazards of televised sessions of legislatures. Comment about the value of the restrictions placed on camera movement in the legislature. Base your essay both on your readings and on your observations of televised sessions of Parliament or your provincial legislature.

4. Evaluate the regulations concerning political broadcasts in Canada. Do you believe that regulations providing for free time, equal time and the distribution of time among major political parties are fair or necessary? Can you suggest changes in the regulations pertaining to political broadcasts?

5. Investigate the regulation of political broadcasting in the United States. In an essay, compare and contrast the way that Canada and the United States regulate political telecasts. Conclude with your appraisal of the merits and demerits of each nation's policies in this area.

"We'll Be Right Back After This Commercial Message!"

Advertising nourishes the consuming power of men. It sets up . . . the goal of a better home, better clothing, better food. . . . It spurs individual exertion and greater production.

SIR WINSTON CHURCHILL

Before the beginning of the fifteenth century most of the people living in Europe and North America lived and worked on farms or in small communities. People knew one another well and interacted on a face-to-face basis. This familiarity made it easy for people to know what others had to offer for sale or trade. There was little need for people to advertise their wares or services. All members of the community knew what was and was not available and from whom.

In the 1700s and early 1800s, a number of technological, economic and social changes combined to create a need for advertising. This period is known as the Industrial Revolution. The Industrial Revolution led to great changes in the lives and work of the people in western Europe and North America. The invention of machines that did the work of many people and of the steam engine that powered the machines led to a dramatic growth in manufacturing and the production of goods to be sold. The manufacturing boom provided more jobs in cities than ever before.

At the same time, technological advances in farming methods reduced the number of jobs available in agriculture. The invention of the reaper, for example, enabled one farmer to do the work of many. The growth of manufacturing and the increasing flow of people from farms and villages to the cities led to a rapid growth in the number and size of cities.

The growth of large cities changed the relationships among

people. People no longer knew most of the people in their city, nor even the people in their neighbourhoods. People did not know the people who wished to sell their goods. In addition, the variety of goods was so vast that choosing among them was difficult. People who wanted to sell their goods needed a way of attracting customers.

The need to make known what products and services were available led to the development of posters. By the 1800s, the poster, used first for church and government notices, had become a common way to advertise.

The growth of the use of machinery and of manufacturing in the cities led to a number of changes in work methods. These changes, too, helped create a need for advertising. Before industrialization the people who produced commodities or performed services were usually the same people who sold those commodities or services.

Industrialization brought about a division of labour. Production was broken up into small, repetitive tasks, and different tasks were assigned to various groups of workers. This division of labour separated the process of the manufacture of goods from the process of the sale of those goods. This split made it necessary for people to advertise their goods and services. The industrial structure that developed and that formed the basis for the economies of the Western nations began to depend on advertising.

Several factors helped to create an atmosphere in which advertising became increasingly necessary. From the nineteenth century the wages and purchasing power of industrial workers steadily increased. The workers spent these wages on the commodities that were becoming available.

Manufacturers encouraged the growing demand for their goods and services by advertising. As industry expanded it became more and more dependent on advertising, both to create sales and then to maintain sales. In time, the economies of the Western

In the 1930s, Canadian consumerism was stimulated by the Eaton's catalogue. Today, television influences consumer demands.

nations came to rely heavily on advertising. It was necessary to advertise in order to maintain levels of consumption. This, in turn, guaranteed the maintenance of industrial production and insured steady employment for workers.

The form of advertisements has always reflected the technology available. As printing became commonplace advertisements were presented in handbills and in newspapers. As radio was perfected, commercial messages became regular features of the broadcast schedule.

The marriage of television and advertising was inevitable. People were ready for television. They were also ready for the consumer goods and services that became available at the end of the Second World War. The changeover of production from war to peacetime purposes created a surplus of consumer goods. Television was a natural tool for advertisers to use. On television, advertisers could combine sound and images to tie people's feelings about their own sense of adequacy, sense of power and attractiveness to their use of the products being advertised.

Sponsorship And Commercial Advertisements

"And, now, a word from our sponsor . . ." was a common announcement during radio programs between 1930 and 1960. Today, when someone on television wants to indicate that the program will be interrupted for an advertisement, he or she often says, "we'll be right back after this commercial message. . . ." The two phrases seem similar, but there are subtle and important differences between the practices indicated by the two phrases.

Sponsorship, a common practice on radio in the 1930s to the 1960s, often meant that an advertiser could control the content of the programs to which the advertiser's name was attached. In

---

■ **Investigation 8.1:** *Speculating About What Elements Make A Successful Television Commercial*

Method:

1. Make a list of your favourite television commercials.

2. Record or discuss the elements that make the commercials appealing to you.

3. Make a list of two or three commercials you find unappealing.

4. Record or discuss the reasons you find the commercials unappealing.

5. Compare your choices of appealing and unappealing commercials with those of other students in the class. Try to identify the common elements that make some commercials appealing and others unappealing.

Skills Developed: **1.26; 2.6; 3.4**

---

a sense, sponsorship indicated censorship or, at least, the possibility of direct control by the advertiser on the program. In radio of the 1940s, for example, a representative of the program's sponsor was often present during a radio broadcast, overseeing the production on behalf of the sponsor.

Sponsorship was also a common practice during the early days of television. Advertisers could select the programs with which they wanted their products associated. American television presented such programs as *Philco Television Playhouse, Goodyear Playhouse, Texaco Star Theatre*, the *Colgate-Palmolive Hour*, and *Hallmark Hall of Fame.* In Canada, sponsors included Ford *(Ford Theatre)*, Frigidaire *(Frigidaire Entertains)*, Burns Meat *(Burns' Chuckwagon)* and General Motors *(G.M. Theatre)*. As in radio, one company sponsored the entire program.

The practice of sponsorship continued during the 1950s and 1960s, although several factors were making the practice less common. Scandals involving several television quiz programs, rising costs of programming, and the increasing complexity of television production and scheduling influenced the change from sponsorship to commercial advertisements.

During the 1960s, some widely watched television quiz programs which were supposed to be genuine contests were shown to have been rigged in favour of one or another contestant. On one show, sponsored by a cosmetics firm, the contestant who was permitted to win had been selected by one of the chief executives of the sponsoring firm.

On commercial television, the revenues made from selling advertising pay most of the costs of television production and provide most of the profits the station makes. The costs of producing television programs rose steadily from the moment television was first introduced. By the late 1960s, the cost of producing a sixty-minute program was as high as $500 000. Single sponsors were finding it too costly to support an entire program.

At the same time, television broadcasters were realizing that they could obtain the costs of production plus higher profits if they sold advertising time in sixty-second or thirty-second seg ments to several advertisers rather than selling the block of time to one sponsor. For a program valued at $500 000, for example, the broadcasters could sell six sixty-second periods for approximately $85 000 each.

One of the advantages of selling advertising time rather than complete sponsorship was a reduction in the influence of sponsors. By the mid-1970s the sale of time for advertising had become the chief form of financing production on most commercial stations. While sponsorship still exists for some afternoon soap operas and for some television specials, it is much less common today than it was during the 1950s and 1960s.

How A Television Commercial Is Made

An advertisement is designed to promote a product, a service or an idea; it is aimed at informing, influencing or persuading people. An advertisement must first capture the viewer's attention and then gain the viewer's interest. Producing an interesting television commercial requires the well-coordinated efforts of people who possess considerable creative and managerial talent. Without their talent, the large sums of money advertisers pay for television commercial messages would be wasted.

The following is an account of the way one commercial message was prepared. The steps outlined are based on fact. However, the company names have been fictionalized; neither Jeansellers Limited nor the Portsmouth Advertising Agency actually exist. Nevertheless, the steps outlined below are typical of many real situations.

During the 1970s, Jeansellers Limited, a Western Canadian chain of retail stores, developed a loyal set of customers for its products among young people between twelve and thirty years of age. Part of the company's success was due to its ability to sell a product people wanted. Another factor was Jeansellers' ability to keep its company name before young people by using television advertising.

By the late 1970s several things had become evident to the executives at Jeansellers. They recognized that they could increase company profits by expanding, making their product available throughout the country. They also recognized the need for an advertising campaign which would make their name as well known throughout the rest of Canada as it was in Western Canada.

Many companies hire advertising agencies to develop and produce their advertisements for television and to plan and purchase from television stations the best possible times to show the advertisement. Jeansellers Limited's advertising account was with the Portsmouth Advertising Agency.

At Portsmouth, the customary practice is to assign an advertiser's account to an **account group** made up of people with specific responsibilities. The Jeansellers' account is assigned to an account group made up of an account executive, creative director, media director, writer/producer and art director. Each of the people in the account group is responsible for a different set of tasks, but the group typically uses a team approach, stressing the strengths of each person.

The **account executive's** first responsibility is to serve as the main point of contact between a client, such as Jeansellers, and the advertising agency. It is the account executive's job to see that the client's wishes are clearly communicated to the other members of the account group.

The account executive must also coordinate the efforts of the account group. To do these tasks, the account executive must understand all aspects of the advertising process and be able to work well with others.

The **creative director** is mainly responsible for translating the client's ideas or wishes into a set of words and images that will please the client and that will communicate with the people at whom the commercial is aimed. The creative director is usually a person who can use words skillfully and create interesting visual images.

The **media director** is part statistician, part historian and part financial expert. He or she is responsible for studying the statistics gathered from surveys, questionnaires, interviews and other market research in order to plan where to place the client's commercial in order to reach the largest audience with the greatest frequency. It is the media director who will spend most of the client's money.

The media director buys advertising time in markets where

the client wants the product to be seen or read about. About 80% of most advertising budgets is spent on "media buys" such as television time. The remaining 20% is spent on producing the commercial message.

The **writer** has the main responsibility for developing the script for the commercial. Like any other writer for film and television, the writer responsible for a television commercial begins with a rough idea, often provided by the creative director. Through several stages, the writer develops the idea into a completely detailed script. In advertising, the writer often works closely with the art director. The **art director** is responsible for planning how to achieve the greatest visual impact with the commercial message.

In advertising agencies, the **producer** is responsible for translating the words and images planned by the creative director, the writer and the art director into a film production. The producer hires all of the people responsible for creating and acting in the commercial. At Portsmouth Agency, the writer is also the producer.

The Portsmouth Agency's work began with information provided by the Jeansellers' president. She told the agency that Jeansellers planned to expand nationally and that the company wanted to make its name as well known in Eastern Canada as it was in the West. The company was prepared to spend a maximum of $500 000 for a Canada-wide television campaign timed to coincide with the opening of new Jeansellers' stores on the Prairies and in Eastern Canada. Because Jeansellers had had previously successful experiences with Portsmouth, the company's president sought suggestions from the agency about the commercial and its distribution.

The account group at Portsmouth agency looked at the Jeansellers' account to identify certain desirable goals in addition to those which the Jeansellers' executive had chosen. As if working on a geometry problem, the members of the account group wanted

Making commercials, like dramatic television programs, requires complex technical equipment.

to set out what they thought were the "givens" of the problem before proceeding to its solution.

The account group reviewed the past campaigns Portsmouth had conducted for Jeansellers. In years past, Jeansellers had run campaigns featuring dancers wearing the company's jeans while they performed to a jingle with a disco beat. The creative people at Portsmouth, especially the writer/producer, recognized that disco music had become less popular with the main audience for the commercial. A decision was made that the new advertisement would introduce a jingle with a more popular beat, making more use of electric guitars and saxophones.

At this time, the writer developed the idea of using the company's jeans as part of a scene in which the viewer is shown how a commercial jingle is recorded. The writer decided to choose performers with whom the viewers could identify. The presentation would focus on young people doing things they enjoyed doing, being creative in their work. It would simply be incidental that the people shown in the commercial would be wearing Jeansellers' jeans.

As the idea took shape, the art director and writer began to develop other ideas which would appeal to the young viewers toward whom the commercial would be aimed. The writer and art director reasoned that the young people who were the largest proportion of Jeansellers' customers were also interested in video games, stereo systems and home computers. They decided that, in addition to showing young people enjoying their work, the commercial would have a "high technology" atmosphere.

These ideas were approved by the account executive and creative director. A decision was then made to produce a demonstration of the commercial for the president of Jeansellers. Portsmouth wanted approval from Jeansellers before proceeding with the production of a commercial.

The producer hired a company specializing in writing music

for commercials to produce a jingle with a new beat for Jean-sellers. At the same time, the producer also hired a film production company to help make the demonstration. It was decided that the demonstration would consist of a slide-tape presentation of the main visuals and the new jingle.

The presentation, costing $500, was shown to the president of Jeansellers. With her approval, the producer contracted for the musical, film, and editing work necessary to produce the commercial.

While the commercial was being produced, the media director planned the purchase of about $450 000 worth of television time. The purchase involved two blocks of time. The first block was a set of times spread over six weeks during the early part of the Fall television season when students were returning to school. The second block was a four-week period immediately preceding Christmas.

The presentation of the commercial was unique. During the first two weeks, a sixty-second version of the commercial was shown. During the remaining weeks, a thirty-second version — the most common length of television commercials — was shown. This type of presentation allowed viewers to become more involved in the commercial than they might have if only a thirty-second version had been shown.

From the time that the president of Jeansellers first approached Portsmouth about the creation of a new commercial to its final showing just before Christmas 1980, fifteen months had passed. During that time more than eighty people had been involved in the production of the commercial and $500 000 had been spent.

Advertising Sales On Television

The selling of advertising time on television is a somewhat complicated affair. Simply put, advertisers pay for time in relation to

We often forget that . . . the primary function of television is that of a merchant . . . people forget that if gun play and neurotic families sell more detergents than classical drama and documentaries on saving our landscape, they'll get gun play and serials.

ALISTAIR COOKE, *U.S. News & World Report*

the size of the audience attracted to the program. This means that television stations charge higher fees for time during or next to programs with larger audiences than for time during or next to shows with smaller audiences. In Canada the Broadcasting Act basically permits a maximum of twelve minutes of advertising time per hour.

Some people are critical of the relationship between advertising and programming on commercial television. Commercial television depends on advertising to stay in business. Critics maintain that, in an effort to win the large audiences which will bring in the highest advertising revenues, producers attempt to create programs which appeal to the largest possible number of people. This practice, critics suggest, eliminates high quality programs which appeal to smaller audiences. Critics claim that programs on commercial television tend to avoid controversial subjects which may offend viewers or content which will attract specialized audiences such as ballet and Shakespearean theatre.

Variations in the rates charged for different programs and the large numbers of commercials carried on television make the purchase of individual advertising time slots impractical. As a result, advertisers purchase time in blocks or packages.

Advertising agencies are usually responsible for handling an advertiser's account. They purchase time on the advertiser's behalf. An agency might indicate to a station or network that its client is prepared to spend $2 000 000 to purchase time for its product. The station provides a list of available time slots and their different costs per thousand views. After some negotiation, during which some times are selected and others are rejected, an agreement about the amount of time to be purchased and its cost is reached.

Within any given block or advertising package, there might be very different programs, drawing audiences of different sizes. A package might include a popular variety show at a cost of $5000 for a thirty-second commercial, a documentary at a cost of $1000, a football game at $10 000, and a spot on the evening news for $2500. In 1981, the CBC charged its advertisers between $8600 and $11 400 per thirty seconds for *Hockey Night in Canada* depending on whether the game was part of the regular season or the playoffs.

Buying time for television advertising is made more complicated by the fact that television programs often appeal to very different audiences. The people who make up the audience for the *Stanley Cup Playoffs* have different characteristics than the people who make up the audience for *Seeing Things* or *The National*.

The study of social and vital statistics is called **demography**. The word comes from the Greek words *demos*, meaning people, and *graphos*, meaning something drawn or written. Demographers who study the make-up of the audiences for different television shows are capable of identifying characteristics which are of special interest to advertisers.

Women have traditionally been the target for advertisers of "soft goods," products sold in supermarkets and drugstores, because they were seen as the people who made most of the decisions about the purchase of such goods. Men have traditionally been seen as the target audience for "hard goods" such as automobiles, television sets and home computers.

An advertiser wishing to sell a detergent is likely to be more interested in a program with an audience made up of a high percentage of women between the ages of eighteen and sixty-four than in a program with an audience largely made up of men eighteen to sixty-four, even if the two audiences are the same size. Similarly, if the product is a shaving lotion, the advertisers will be more interested in an audience composed mainly of males eighteen to sixty-four than of women in the same age range.

In the 1970s demographic research about audience characteristics became common. Since then, advertisers and television

● Investigation 8.2:

To Determine The Extent To Which Advertisers Use Sexual Stereotyping To Sell Products On Television

Method:

1. Each member of the class select one television advertisement and identify the product being advertised

2. Determine whether the product is aimed primarily at men or at women.

3. Define sexual stereotyping, indicating what you would regard as evidence of stereotypical representations of men and women.

4. Use a form similar to Appendix IX, "A Guide for Analyzing Advertising on Television," to analyze the advertiser's appeal.

5. Pool your results with those of other students and answer the following questions:

a. What proportion of the advertisements used sexual stereotyping to sell products?

b. Are there similarities among the men and women shown in the advertisements with respect to:

(1) aggressiveness/passivity

(2) occupation

(3) age

c. Are men and women equal targets of advertisements using sexual stereotyping to sell a product?

6. Write a letter to an advertiser giving your view about the use of sexual stereotyping in promoting a product.

Skills Developed: **1.11; 1.22; 1.23; 2.5; 3.2; 4.2**

Producers and directors of television programming and commercials sometimes face unusual challenges. In 1939, a Los Angeles television station was considering televising and advertising the nationally famous Pasadena Fall Flower Show. In this photograph, the crew (*left to right*, Jackey Feindel, director, Art Lasky, assistant, Mickey Whelan, operative cameraman, and George Haines, key grip) is experimenting to see how well different flowers will reproduce on television. Among the blossoms carried by Maxine Gray in this strange "audition" were Crysanthemums from China, Catalya Orchids from South America, Hoya Carnosa from Dutch East Indies, Red Orchids from Chile and Brazil, and Bird of Paradise from South Africa. Some of the flowers televised perfectly, while others, because of colour contrasts, lost their beauty in the pictorial broadcast.

executives have focused their attention on getting the "correct" demographic "profile." Programs that don't "deliver" the sex and age audience distribution advertisers want have a more difficult time winning enough advertisers to survive financially than do those programs that do deliver the desired demographics.

Age is an important factor in television advertising. Young people are often concerned about their personal appearance and its effect on members of the opposite sex. Knowing this, advertisers of cosmetics want a large number of young women to watch the programs around and during which their commercials appear. As people age they tend to become more concerned about their health. Thus, advertisers of products designed to increase older people's vitality, regularity, or security are interested in programs appealing to people fifty years of age and older.

Advertising Costs: The Price Of Creativity

Advertising is a costly business. In addition to the costs of buying television time, there are the production costs involved in making commercial advertisements. The American Telephone and Telegraph Company is said to have spent approximately $1 million to produce one thirty-second commercial advertisement designed to persuade people to make more long-distance telephone calls.

The budget to produce a single thirty-second advertisement for one popular soft drink was $50 000 in 1980. If a half hour program was budgeted at the rate of $50 000 per thirty seconds, it would cost more than $2 500 000 to produce!

The emphasis on television advertising has prompted some people to suggest that more creative effort goes into television commercials than into television programs. This may be true because a television program has half an hour or an hour to tell its story, but a good television commercial must tell its story in an attention-grabbing, entertaining fashion in only thirty seconds.

What Advertisers Hope To Accomplish With Television Advertising

The main reason people advertise is to promote the sale of the goods and services they have to offer. Television advertising seeks to accomplish this purpose in a number of ways.

Advertisers try to influence people to want their product or their brand of some product. Some advertisers promote the sales of everyday products that people need and use such as food and

---

Investigation 8.3: | *To Compare The Techniques Used By Advertisers On Television To Appeal To Different Segments Of The Population*

Method:

1. Select three advertisements which are designed to appeal to three different segments of the viewing population. For example, some commercials about hair-colouring solutions are aimed primarily at people who are sensitive about aging. Toy commercials are often aimed at pre-school youngsters. Commercials for food products are often aimed at homemakers.

2. Identify the techniques used by advertisers for each of the three products you have chosen. With your classmates, organize your data for an analysis which will permit you to answer the question: *Do advertisers use different techniques to influence different groups of people?*

Skills Developed: **1.14; 1.15; 1.22; 1.23; 1.26; 2.3**

clothing. Others advertise items that are unrelated to day-to-day living. The desire to have something that isn't prompted by one's day-to-day needs is called **synthetic demand**.

Advertisers often use people's need to feel socially acceptable, their need to feel strong, and their identification with particular groups to sell products. The advertiser does this by pairing the satisfaction of the need with the purchase of the product being advertised. So, for example, an advertisement for a breath mint says: "Having trouble meeting new friends? Maybe it's your breath!" Other commercials imply that the user of the product will be more socially attractive to members of the opposite sex. Thus, one automobile manufacturer's advertisement says: "Girls never noticed me, until I started driving a Dotto!"

According to research, advertisers using the **implied promise technique** described above are least likely to be successful with people who have very poor images of themselves or very positive images of themselves. These people are generally the most difficult to persuade. It is the middle group of people with neither a very poor nor a very positive self-image which is most easily persuaded. It is also this group into which most television viewers fall.

Some advertisers try to impress upon the viewer-consumer that, because some powerful or attractive people use product X, the consumer will be powerful or attractive simply by using Product X. These advertisers seek to associate use of their product with glamourous people, exotic settings, pleasurable activities or symbols. The technique is sometimes called **image advertising**. What the advertisers who use image advertising are selling is the connection between their product and some pleasant image.

Image advertising and advertising using implied promises play on social and psychological conditions that are already present in the society. People want to be liked by others. They want to feel that they can control the situations in which they find themselves. They want to feel positively about themselves. By linking these desires to some product, advertisers hope to entice people to try their product. They are hopeful that once people have tried their product, they will continue to use it.

Some advertisers seek to persuade the viewer to purchase Brand Y rather than Brand Z of some product. To do so, advertisers use a variety of techniques. Some claim superiority for their brand by directly comparing it with another or by implying that it is better than another.

This photograph shows the filming of an early Kellogg's BRAN Flakes advertisement.

Direct comparisons rarely report the results of carefully conducted research. Instead, the viewer is presented with a **testimonial**, a claim of superiority by a knowledgeable user or some authoritative expert. The user or expert is presented to the viewer in such a way that the viewer gets the impression that the user/expert knows what he or she is talking about.

In an advertisement for laundry detergent, the viewer might see a person who says: "I manage a commercial laundry. At one time or another, we've tried them all; but, now we're using Brand A." What the viewer doesn't know is whether Brand A is cheaper, or is more effective or is more attractively packaged than the others. The comparison among brands is implied or indirect.

In the advertisement that says "Four out of five doctors use Brand Y," the superiority of Brand Y to other brands is implied, but not actually stated. It may be that the four out of five doctors use Brand Y because the manufacturer provides them with Brand Y without charging them.

In some advertisements claiming that Brand Z is better, the viewer is never told what Brand Z is better than. If Brand Z is a washing detergent, it may mean that Brand Z is better than using nothing at all, but is about equal to using Brand Y!

It is thought that people are influenced to purchase a product when the product is something that everyone seems to be using. The technique is called the **bandwagon technique**. It seeks to persuade people that since everyone else is buying Brand G, they should be getting on the bandwagon, too. The appeal in this form of advertising is to conformity. Most people don't like to go against the dominant trend unless they have good reasons for their opposition.

The bandwagon technique is sometimes used in combination with others. For example, the slogan "All Canada loves Brand B" uses both the bandwagon technique and a form of image advertising. This slogan appeals to conformity and to the viewer's positive feelings toward Canada.

Plain folks is a technique based on the idea that people will purchase products which they see being used by people who look just like them. The advertiser is really saying to the viewer that ordinary people just like the viewer are buying the product, implying that the viewer should be buying it, too.

Does Advertising Promote Sales?

Surprising as it may seem, there is very little direct evidence that television advertising actually leads people to buy the products being advertised. Nevertheless, advertisers continue to spend large sums of money to put their products in front of television viewers.

Psychologists who have studied the process of changing people's attitudes are able to cast some light on the effectiveness of advertising. Although persuading people to buy something and persuading people to change their attitudes toward something are different, there is enough similarity between the two processes to make use of what psychologists have learned in order to understand television advertising.

Psychologists have discovered that face-to-face contact is the most effective way to persuade people to change their minds about some issue or topic. When it comes to less direct forms of communication, no one way of communicating has proven consistently better than any other form of communication.

A variety of factors seem to influence the process by which people can be persuaded to change their minds about something. Among those factors are the presence or absence of messages which contradict one another, the characteristics of the viewer who is receiving the message, and the amount of repetition. Examining those factors that can be controlled by the advertiser, a few patterns can be observed.

Using attractive and authoritative sources to sell products has been a common practice on television for many years. As a general rule, attractive sources are better than authoritative sources. An authoritative source is one which has some expert status. Such sources as doctors, judges, lawyers and teachers are often considered to be authoritative because they have spent many years studying. However, for the authoritative source to be most persuasive, the source must state a well-constructed argument.

Attractive sources do not have to present well-constructed arguments. Attractive sources are generally more believable than authoritative sources. People tend to believe sources with which they are familiar, which they like, which are attractive and which they think are similar to themselves.

In addition to expertise and attractiveness, there are a number of other factors which make a source believable. These factors include trustworthiness, humour, and clarity of speech. Sources which agree with the viewer's point of view will be considered by that viewer to be more believable. If the message disagrees with the viewpoint of the person watching, the person will be less likely to think the source is believable.

When people have already formed an opinion about something, they will tend to seek out information which supports their point of view. If a viewer has just purchased a Brand S automobile, the viewer will pick out information from advertisements which support the viewer's decision, showing why the choice was a good one. The viewer will probably be less open to information which implies that the decision about the automobile was a wrong one.

In recent years, commercials have made more use of humour than in the past. However, to date, there has been comparatively little research done on the effectiveness of the use of humour in advertising.

One problem with humour that pokes fun at somebody or something is that the viewer may be upset or annoyed. The viewer

■ Investigation 8.4: *To Identify How Television Commercials Influence Consumer Behaviour*

Method:

1. Select one product advertised on television which you would like to have. In a paragraph, explain why you would like to have the product. In developing your paragraph, you may wish to consider the following: *Did you want the product because*

a. the advertisement made the product seem attractive?

b. other people or media had informed you about the product?

c. you had used the product on other occasions and you were convinced of its usefulness and/or attractiveness?

2. Observe a number of television commercials. Identify the techniques used by the advertisers to sell their products. How many techniques are used in a single commercial? Which techniques are most often used? Are some techniques more consistently associated with a particular product line? Speculate about the effectiveness of the advertising techniques used for influencing purchasing habits.

3. Compare the way a single product (for example, home computers) is treated by various media (television, magazines, radio, newspapers). Is the same product advertised using different persuasive techniques in different media? Select the advertisement and medium you think is the most successful in persuading the consumer to purchase the product. Explain why you think it is the most effective.

Skills Developed: **1.24; 1.26; 2.3; 2.7; 3.1; 3.2; 3.5; 4.4** may identify with the object of the humour or may possess the article being made the butt of the joke. If the advertisement pokes fun at people who wear yellow ski hats, for example, and the viewer wears a yellow ski hat, the viewer may feel ridiculed. The product which the advertiser wants to promote probably won't get a favourable reaction from this viewer.

Making people fearful can change their point of view about an issue. However, producing great amounts of fear only makes people anxious and rarely affects their purchasing behaviour. Thus, messages for home security products which are particularly frightening may have less influence on sales than more moderate presentations.

How Television Advertising Influences Children

It is estimated that, through all media, a modern family is confronted with no less than 1450 advertisements a day.

MAX BRAITHWAITE, "Advertising Through The Mass Media," in *Coping With The Mass Media*

People are especially concerned about the impact of television advertising on children. Because children are young and have not yet had much "education," they are thought to be particularly vulnerable to television advertising. That is why some networks, such as the CBC, prohibit advertising during or between programs aimed at children. Others have rules which apply to what may or may not be advertised and the form the advertising may take.

Concern about the impact of television advertising on children has led to many studies. The findings of the studies provide valuable information about how children are influenced by television advertising.

Young children (5-8 years old) sometimes say that commercials are different from programs because commercials are "funnier" or "shorter" than programs. Older children (9-12 years old) are able to make more meaningful distinctions. For example, they point out that programs are supposed to entertain people and that commercials are trying to sell things.

Older children are better able to recognize that selling is the main purpose of television advertising. Many children, especially those younger than seven years of age, do not seem as able to recognize that television advertising is trying to persuade them to buy certain products.

People who are critical of advertising directed at children express concern about the large number of commercials children see on television. They are also concerned about the effects of seeing the same commercials over and over again.

According to the evidence available, exposure to many commercials does create more favourable attitudes toward advertising and advertised products, but it does not influence how well children understand commercials. So far as researchers can tell, seeing the same commercial over and over again does not make its message any more persuasive.

Those concerned about television advertising have succeeded in convincing advertisers to include specific information in their advertisements. Called **product disclaimers**, the information might state that "batteries are not included," or that the clothing worn by dolls in an advertisement is sold separately at additional cost.

Research has shown that the form of these product disclaimers has an impact on a child's ability to recall the disclaimer. Disclaimers which are spoken and also presented in written form on the screen are better remembered than disclaimers which are only shown on the screen. Simply worded disclaimers are better understood than disclaimers which are complicated.

The effects of food advertising directed at children is well documented. It has been shown that children learn the information contained in food advertisements. They tend to believe the claims made for the food advertised and anticipate benefits from having the food. Children who see the food advertisements which are

■ **Investigation 8.5:**	*To Make A Fifteen-second Commercial Message*

Method:

1.   Select a product or service to advertise in a fifteen-second commercial message. Investigate the product or service carefully, learning as much as you can about its purposes, characteristics and limitations. If the product selected is imaginary, develop its purpose and characteristics before beginning Step Two.

2.   Identify the major purposes and elements in the commercial message you wish to deliver, using the following outline:

a. purpose or main message of the commercial
b. sequence outline of commercial
c. character profiles
d. location/setting of commercial

3.   Prepare a shooting script for the commercial, using the sequence outline as a guide.

4.   Using the character profiles, cast the characters who will appear in your commercial.

5.   Develop a storyboard for your commercial, illustrating shot selection and camera angles.

6.   Rehearse the commercial.

7.   If there is videotaping equipment available, prepare a videotape of your commercial. If such equipment is not available, present your commercial to the class as a live "drama."

8.   Conduct a class discussion of the commercial.

9.   Prepare a short essay documenting this experience. In addition to describing the experience carefully, your essay should explain your reactions to the various parts of the process of developing a commercial message.

Skills Developed: **1.11; 1.12; 1.13; 1.14; 2.3; 2.4; 3.1; 3.3** aimed at them tend to influence their parents to buy the foods advertised.

As a group, parents are to some extent negative toward advertising aimed at children. However, when parents are asked whether they are in favour of banning commercials, if a ban would result in eliminating children's programs, the parents usually say "no".

Test Yourself

A. *Identification:* Explain the meaning and/or significance of the following in your own words:

sponsorship	account group
account executive	creative director
media director	demography
synthetic demand	implied promise
testimonial	bandwagon technique
plain folks	product disclaimer

B. *True And False:* Indicate with the letter T or the letter F whether you think the following statements are accurate or inaccurate. If any part of the statement is false or inaccurate, use the letter F.

1. The presence of advertising on television increases people's desire to consume goods.

2. The selling of small segments of time to advertisers results in less influence over program content by the advertiser than was the case with sponsorship.

3. Viewer age is more important than viewer sex in determining the placement of an advertisement on television.

4. The desire to attract and keep advertisers may lead producers to avoid controversial subjects on their programs.

5. Television commercials cannot influence people to buy something they do not want.

6. Many advertisers play on viewer insecurities to try to influence them to purchase their products.

7. People with low self-concepts are easier to influence than viewers with high self-esteem.

8. Testimonial advertisements always provide the viewer with specific information about the products compared.

9. The number of times an advertisement runs is more important than the content of the advertisement in determining the advertisement's influence on the viewer.

10. Viewers are more easily persuaded to buy products when the advertisement includes the testimonial of an expert than when the advertisement shows attractive people.

11. Children under the age of twelve are unable to understand the commercial intention of advertisements.

C. *Multiple Choice:* For each question indicate which response you think best answers the question.

1. Which of the following factors helped lead to the development of advertising?
   a. the growth of cities
   b. the development of moveable type
   c. the growth of large corporations
   d. the invention of electronic mass media

2. The concept of sponsorship of television programs declined because:

    a. audiences resented the influence companies had over program content.

    b. audiences tired of seeing many commercials for the same product on one program.

    c. advertisers preferred to advertise in other media.

    d. sponsors were embarrassed by a series of quiz show scandals.

3. The task of planning when and where an advertising campaign will be run on television belongs to:

    a. the creative director.

    b. the account executive.

    c. the media director.

    d. the account group.

4. The cost of a thirty-second slot of advertising time is determined by:

    a. the time of day the advertisement appears.

    b. the number of viewers expected to see the commercial.

    c. the size of the company purchasing the advertising time.

    d. the theme of the program on which the advertisement will run.

5. Demography refers to:

    a. the characteristics of the viewing audience.

    b. the product likes and dislikes of the viewing audience.

    c. the distribution of an advertisement over a variety of program types.

    d. the measurement of the degree of success of an advertising campaign.

6. Image advertising:

    a. makes a product appear better than it really is.

    b. makes viewers identify with glamorous people who are seen using or promoting a product.

c. makes viewers think they will become more successful, attractive and important if they use the product.

d. plays on viewers' lack of self-confidence to make them purchase a product.

7. An advertisement showing a well-known athlete using or promoting a product is an example of:

   a. an image advertisement.

   b. a bandwagon advertisement.

   c. a synthetic demand.

   d. a testimonial.

8. A viewer will most likely respond positively to an advertisement:

   a. if the viewpoint expressed in the advertisement is similar to that of the viewer.

   b. if the advertisement contains humour.

   c. if the message of the advertisement presents information that contradicts information presented in competitors' advertisements.

   d. if the advertisement introduces information that was previously not known by the viewer.

9. There is a danger in using humour to sell products because:

   a. the humour may unintentionally poke fun at the product.

   b. the humour may unintentionally poke fun at the viewer.

   c. many viewers do not have a sense of humour.

   d. when viewers laugh they miss the remainder of the commercial message.

10. Critics are concerned about advertising on children's television programs because:

    a. children are encouraged to spend their money on products they do not need.

    b. the products advertised on children's programs are often of poor quality.

    c. children are often unable to understand the intention behind television advertisements.

    d. children put pressure on their parents to buy them everything they see on television.

D. *Activities For Further Investigation*

1. Prepare an essay indicating your agreement or disagreement with the following statement: " . . . more creative effort goes into advertisements than into television programs."

2. In both movies and television, successful efforts are often imitated in an effort to benefit from a popular trend. Such imitations are called "spin-offs." Is the spin-off syndrome evident in the world of television commercials? Identify any recurring themes and styles evident in television commercials you have viewed. Provide examples of spin-off advertisements. Analyze the reasons for the success of such advertisements.

3. To what extent have political advertisements adopted the techniques and values of advertisements for consumer products? In an essay, analyze the similarities and differences between political advertisements and consumer advertisements.

4. Debate the following: Resolved: Commercials should be banned from all programming directed toward children.

5. In some countries, nationally operated television networks are commercial free. In Canada, pay television is free of commercials other than those which promote upcoming programs. Debate the following: Resolved: All television should be commercial free.

6. A number of advertising techniques have been described in this book, including synthetic demand, implied promise, bandwagon, and so forth. Which of the techniques do you find most and which least persuasive? Identify the elements of each that you believe account for the success or failure of the technique.

7. Invite a spokesperson from CTV or CBC to address your class on the topic of network policy on childrens' programming. Prepare questions in advance of the guest's visit.

The English-language Media And Canadian Identity

The American Challenge

A nation's identity is transmitted by its media of mass communication. In order to ensure a vital culture, a people must be able to communicate with one another about their impressions of the lives they live. We stated in Chapter One that it is misleading to assume that observations about the impact of television on one linguistic group apply to members of other linguistic groups and that the focus in this book was on the impact of television on English-speaking Canadians. In English-speaking Canada, there is a growing concern that the messages being communicated through its media do not reflect the English-speaking Canadian experience. The concern is that English-speaking Canada is being engulfed by American cultural symbols, practices, and values.

For many years, it was thought that English-speaking Canadians preferred American television programs and that they seldom watched programs produced in Canada. The true picture is more complicated. Table 9.1 reports the percentage of **broadcast time** and the percentage of **viewing time** of various types of Canadian and foreign programming on English-language television for the years 1979 and 1980.

From Table 9.1, it can be seen that of all the programs *aired* or *broadcast* on the English-language television system, 33% were Canadian produced and 67% were foreign produced. Comparing

Table 9.1: *Percentage of broadcast and viewing time for various types of Canadian and foreign programming on English-language television, 1979-1980*

| | Broadcast Time | | Viewing Time | |
	% Canadian	% Foreign	% Canadian	% Foreign
All Programs	33	67	26	74
News	62	38	89	11
Public Affairs	67	33	71	29
Sports	60	40	79	21
Drama	4	96	3	97
Variety/Music/Quiz	31	69	20	80

Source: Adapted from *CBC Annual Report 1980-81*, p. 8.

these figures with the distribution of the time *viewers spent watching television*, it can be seen that English-speaking Canadians spent 26% of their viewing time watching Canadian-produced programs and 74% of their time watching foreign-produced programs. Thus, for the English-language television system, the proportion of time Canadians spent viewing the two categories of programs was quite close to the amount of broadcast time devoted to each.

This general pattern prevailed for all types of programming. Of the broadcast time on English-language television that was devoted to news, 62% was Canadian-produced. Canadians spent 89% of the time they devoted to viewing news watching Canadian-produced news programs and 11% of their news-viewing time watching foreign-produced news. For public affairs, 67% was Canadian produced and 33% foreign produced. Canadians spent 71% of their public affairs viewing time watching Canadian-produced programs and 29% watching foreign-produced programs.

Table 9.2 shows how Canadians distributed their viewing time by program types in the years 1979 to 1980. Canadians spent approximately 50% of their television viewing time watching dramatic programs, 18% watching variety/music/quiz programs, 10% watching the news, 8% watching sports, 6% watching public affairs, and 8% watching programs that did not fall into these categories.

Table 9.2: *Distribution of Canadian English-language Television Viewing, 1979-1980*

Program Type	Percentage of Total Viewing Time
Drama	50%
Variety/Music/Quiz	18%
News	10%
Sports	8%
Public Affairs	6%
Other	8%
All Program Types	100%

Source: Adapted from *CBC ANNUAL REPORT 1980-81*, p. 8

Table 9.1 shows that 4% of all the time devoted to broadcasting drama was devoted to Canadian-produced dramatic programs and 96% to foreign-produced programs. The distribution of viewing time for dramatic programs was of a similar proportion. Canadians spent 3% of their drama viewing time watching Canadian-produced dramatic programs and 97% of their drama viewing time watching foreign-produced dramatic shows. Since Canadians spend 50% of their *total viewing time* watching drama and since most drama is foreign produced, it is not surprising that

Although Canada is the single most lucrative foreign market for the products of Burbank and Television City, virtually all U.S. television programs are written and produced with only the gigantic U.S. market in mind. This is the fundamental reason why the entertainment programming of Canadian television channels so often seems to be an inaccurate reflection of the Canadian cultural reality.

PIERRE JUNEAU, President, Canadian Broadcasting Corporation, "Making Canadians Visible," in *Multiculturalism: Visible Minorities & the Media Conference Report*, 1982 people have had the somewhat misleading impression that Canadians prefer to watch foreign (particularly American)-produced programs.

When a culture's symbols, practices, and values are not shown on a nation's media, the culture will erode. The amount of exposure American content gets in the English-language media in Canada has led to the establishment of Canadian content regulations. These regulations state the minimum amount of Canadian material that must be carried on Canadian radio and television.

In a similar vein, tax legislation encourages the Canadian publishing and film industries. For example, advertisers receive tax benefits for placing advertisements in Canadian- rather than foreign-owned publications. Canadians who invest in Canadian feature films are able to deduct from their taxes virtually the entire amount of their investment. There are also tax laws that discourage both foreign enterprise from investing in Canada and Canadians from investing their capital outside of Canada.

Government-supported agencies seek to offset foreign cultural influence by encouraging Canadian artists and writers. The Canada Council provides grants to Canadian writers, artists, academics, dance companies and theatre groups. Documentaries, animations and other short film subjects produced by the National Film Board of Canada have won praise for Canadian filmmakers worldwide. The Canadian Film Development Corporation provides government subsidies for Canadian feature filmmakers.

Whether these regulations and agencies have lessened the impact of American images on English-speaking Canadians is not clear. Some Canadians fear that American cultural values are still overwhelming English-language Canadian culture. Others insist that there is no essential difference between Canadian and American values. Yet others say that cross-cultural contact is an inevitable, and good, part of the development of every culture.

C'EST VOTRE BIBLIOTHÈQUE

ΑΥΤΗ ΕΙΝΑΙ Η ΒΙΒΛΙΟΘΗΚΗ ΣΑΣ

這是你們的圖書館

QUESTA È LA VOSTRA BIBLIOTECA

ESTA ES SU BIBLIOTECA

ISTO É A SUA BIBLIOTECA

DIES IST IHRE BÜCHEREI

EZ AZ ÖN KÖNYVTÁRA

TO JEST WASZA BIBLIOTEKA

ЦЕ ВАША БІБЛІОТЕКА

Does English-language Television Accurately Portray The Canadian Mosaic?

In these final days of the twentieth century, television, more than any other medium, holds up the mirror in which Canadian society can see itself reflected. The television pictures are vital: they are in colour. Today 11 million television sets carry messages and reinforce the values of 24 million Canadians.

SALOME BEY, singer, actress, Black Canadian, "The Minority Viewpoint," in *Multiculturalism: Visible Minorities & The Media Conference Report*, 1982

Some cultural groups in Canada are faced with a dual threat — the invasion of American culture and the lack of representation of their own culture on Canadian television. An important aspect of the relationship between television and culture is the extent to which Canadian television programming accurately reflects the cultural diversity of Canadian society. Many cultural groups in Canada maintain that English-language television reflects the cultural bias of white, Anglo and middle-class Canadians.

The constant presence of certain groups on television or the marked absence of others may influence people to believe that certain groups are more valued or less valued by society. For example, when young children of a particular cultural group fail to see or rarely see members of that group on television, they may feel that the group to which they belong isn't considered very important. This, in turn, may influence how these children view themselves.

If the members of a certain group are shown, but always in a negative way, members of this group may come to regard themselves negatively, too. For example, if children of group X see members of their group always portrayed on television as mean-spirited, they may begin to believe that all members of group X — including themselves — are mean-spirited. The practice also strengthens the prejudices of those who possess negative attitudes toward the members of group X.

A study of the prime time programs and newscasts offered on the English-language CBC and CTV networks was conducted during the week of April 1 to April 9, 1980, for the Multiculturalism Directorate, Secretary of State. The study was titled *The Portrayal*

The Parliament of Canada accepted Multiculturalism as official government policy in 1971, guaranteeing the cultural freedom and equality of all Canadians.

In 1982, Multiculturalism was entrenched in the Charter of Rights and Freedoms, part of Canada's new Constitution.

So ours is officially, as well as in fact, a multicultural, multiracial society.

But anyone from abroad watching Canadian television, or perusing the printed media, could justifiably conclude this is an almost pure white society.

For Canada's visible minorities, the Blacks, the Chinese, the Japanese, the Asians, whether born here or elsewhere, are mostly invisible in the Canada seen through our media. They're seldom portrayed as if they belonged here.

The Government of Canada has therefore adopted a policy of representative depiction of visible and ethnic minorities in all federal government advertising and communications and Treasury Board has issued guidelines to all federal departments and agencies.

This booklet aims to assist public servants in knowing, understanding and applying the guidelines to ensure that the multiracial and multicultural composition of Canada is fully reflected in all communications, both internal and external.

Although all forms of government communications are covered by the guidelines, advertising and the media merit special attention.

"If we are not accurately seen in the mirror the media holds up to society, then, clearly, we are somehow not part of that society." Salome Bey

The opening pages from *Visible Minorities in Government Communications: A MATTER OF BALANCE*. Produced by Multiculturalism Canada, Office of the Secretary of State, the booklet was designed to help public servants understand and apply the federal government's policy of "representative depiction of visible and ethnic minorities in all federal government advertising and communications."

▪ Investigation 9.1:

To Evaluate The Extent To Which English-language Television Presents Stereotypic Views Of The Members Of Cultural Groups

Method:

1. Each student in the class select a different television dramatic program in which the central characters' cultural backgrounds are evident.

2. Using a characterization check list similar to Appendix V, systematically record the attributes the central characters exhibit.

3. Prepare your data for presentation to the class.

4. Develop a statement stating how television presents the members of various cultural groups. Are the members of some groups always associated with particular characteristics?

5. Discuss why television programmers present members of different groups as they do. Why are some cultural groups poorly represented on television? What does the presentation of cultural groups tell you about Canadian society? About television's role in society?

Skills Developed: **2.5; 2.6; 3.1; 3.2; 3.4; 4.3; 4.4**

---

of Canadian Cultural Diversity on English-Language Canadian Network Television.

The analysis of the fifteen hours of prime time programming showed that recognizable cultural groups were rarely present on English-language Canadian network television. More than 90% of the characters shown on the entertainment programs analyzed were characterized as white North Americans. Table 9.3 shows the proportion of cultural groups portrayed on the programs in the study.

Table 9.3: *Proportion of Cultural Groups Shown in Fifteen Hours of Prime Time English-language Television on the CBC and CTV Networks During the Period April 1 to April 9, 1980*

Cultural Group	Percentage of All Characters Presented
American	59.1
English Canadian	24.0
Italian	5.0
Native Indian	3.0
British	2.2
Eastern European	2.2
French Canadian	2.0
Chinese	0.5
Swedish	0.5
Greek	0.5
African	0.5
Asian	0.5
Total	100.0

Source: G. Teachman, *The Portrayal of Canadian Cultural Diversity on English-Language Canadian Network Television: A Content Analysis* (Toronto, PEAC Developments, 1980)

The small number of characters other than white North Americans made it difficult to see many general patterns among the roles and the characteristics of the few members of those minority cultures that were portrayed. There were, however, a few noticeable patterns. It was observed that in dramatic programs white characters were seen as coming from more affluent backgrounds than non-white characters and that in only one case was a non-white character portrayed in a hero role. However, the minority cultural groups portrayed were generally neither stereotyped nor the object of overt negative references.

There are approximately 85 ethno-cultural groups in Canada.

In the seven hours of newscasts analyzed in the study, over 85% of the news items contained only white, English-speaking Canadians or Americans. In the remaining 15% of the news items, the people presented were from Britain, Iran, Italy, Egypt, China, Afghanistan, Vietnam, Israel, Puerto Rico and Switzerland.

Only a very small percentage of the news items in the study dealt with events or people from other than North American backgrounds. This made it difficult to pick out many patterns. However, in the majority of news items containing people from non-North American backgrounds, there were few detectable biases or negative connotations. Only five news items contained obvious bias. For example, in an item from Britain, the term "crowd of angry blacks" was used to describe a crowd that contained both whites and blacks.

Many Canadians argue that English-language television ignores or misrepresents working-class and rural Canadians as well as minority cultural groups. In an analysis of the background of the 123 news announcers presented on camera, it was observed that all appeared to be North American. Most of these announcers were white and male. At the time of the study, all sports and weather items were reported by males. Those women who were presented appeared to be younger than the males and more often were reporting local news.

According to the study, English-language Canadian television did not present a statistically accurate distribution of its cultural or economic groups on prime time programs. The authors state:

> The over-representation of the white male found in the present study may not be a deliberate distortion of reality, but may instead reflect the esteem given in our social value system to the power this segment of society has over others.

The authors of the study also suggest that the absence of cultural subgroups may reflect attitudes toward cultural and economic

■ **Investigation 9.2:**	*To Determine Whether Television Accurately Describes The Scope And Nature Of Work In Canadian Society*

Method:

1. Select one Canadian television dramatic program as a focus for this investigation.

2. Identify the occupations of the main characters in the program.

3. On the basis of your observations, answer the following questions:

a. Are the characters shown doing their work on the program or does all of their work take place off camera?

b. How important is their work in the lives of the characters?

4. Pool your observations with those made by other students in the class. List all of the occupations observed by class members and put them into the categories listed in step 5.

5. Compare the distribution of occupations observed on television with those of all Canadians:

> Agriculture 4.7%
> Forestry 0.8%
> Fishing and trapping 0.2%
> Mining 1.6%
> Manufacturing 19.6%
> Construction 6.3%
> Transportation, communication and utilities 8.6%
> Trade 17.4%
> Finance, insurance and real estate 5.5%
> Service 28.2%
> Public administration 7.1%

6. Does television accurately depict the variety and distribution of work in Canadian society?

7.   Should television programmers be concerned that television present an accurate picture of Canadian society? What are possible consequences of presenting a distorted image of Canadian society?

Skills Developed: 1.13; 1.22; 3.4; 4.2; 4.3; 4.6

A high school student spends an enormous amount of time in front of a television set and will have watched 350 000 commercials by the time he graduates. If visible minorities are not part of this electronic panorama, how are young people going to accept Blacks, Asians or Native people as part of their Canadian world?

THE HONOURABLE JIM FLEMING, Minister of State — Multiculturalism, "Opening Address," in *Multiculturalism: Visible Minorities & The Media Conference Report*, 1982

minorities in Canada at the time of the study. They point out as well that "the danger exists that negative attitudes may be created or reinforced through this low representation [of minority cultural and economic group members] on television."

Another question about the relationship between television and culture involves the presentation of cultural groups in television advertising. This question was investigated in a study conducted between May 25 and May 28 and on June 2, 1977, and involved an analysis of television advertising on four Canadian channels. The study, by Lateef Owaisi and Zafar Bangash, entitled *Visible Minorities in Mass Media Advertising*, was prepared for the Executive of the Canadian Consultative Council in Multiculturalism. Although there have been some changes since this report was completed, the patterns outlined in the study still prevail on Canadian television in the 1980s.

In the study, emphasis was given to advertisements which used performers. Just over 2000 people appeared in the television advertisements during the period of study. Of the 2064 people, only 48 could be considered members of visible minority groups. There were 24 blacks and 24 Asians. If advertisements for charity organizations and advertisements made in the United States were to be excluded, there would be only 20 commercials in which a visible minority was shown. The authors of the study point out:

> The bulk of visible minority group representation, blacks as well as Asians, is the role of hungry, needy people receiving handouts from

Investigation 9.3:   *To Evaluate The Extent To Which Television Presents A Stereotypic Portrayal Of Older People*

Method:

1. Make a list of five people over the age of 65 with whom you are personally acquainted. Below each person's name, make a list of characteristics you associate with the individual. Keep the descriptions brief, using one or two words for each character trait.

2. Make a list of five characters over the age of 65 whom you have seen on television. Draw your characters from television drama, comedies and commercials. Identify the character traits of the older people seen on television in the same way that you did for the older people you personally know.

3. Based on your two lists, compare the people you know with the television characters.

a. What are the most common characteristics portrayed by older people on television?

b. What are the similarities and differences between the television characters and the people you personally know? Do the television characters exhibit as varied characteristics as the people you know?

c. What do you think is the impact of the treatment given to older people on television?

d. Why do you think television presents older people in the way that it does?

e. Are there some forms of television (drama, comedy or commercials) that present a more accurate or less accurate image of older people than the other forms?

4. Write a letter to one of the major television networks or to the producer of a specific program stating your concerns about the portrayal of older people on television.

Skills Developed: 1.11; 1.13; 1.22; 1.24; 1.25; 1.26; 3.2; 3.4; 4.4; 4.6

whites. Such stereotyping appears to be the dominant feature of visible minority group representation in television commercials.

The authors quote a representative of the Association of Canadian Radio and Television Artists (ACTRA) as saying:

> When commercials are made in Canada, demand for Anglo-Saxon models and performers is much greater [than models from other groups]. That is why they are all over; it is white, wall to wall! It is much easier for people with English accents to get commercial assignments than any other groups. In a descending order, blacks follow the whites in demand, followed by Asians. For native Indians, it is extremely difficult to get a job except where there are stereotype roles in western films or filming parts of Northern Ontario.

The subtle influence of what people see on television on their attitudes is not well known. It is nevertheless the case that the constant repetition of certain images and themes can supply people with inaccurate views of society.

Many English-speaking Canadians insist that they should have the opportunity to choose from the broadest selection of offerings in film, music, literature, television, and other forms of cultural expression. They believe that their choice should not be limited by considerations of Canadian or foreign content. Others believe that the threat posed by foreign cultural influences is so serious that Canadians must be exposed to Canadian culture and must be limited in their access to foreign influences.

Federal media policy is based on the belief that Canadian culture will be threatened if government does not both encourage Canadian cultural expression and limit the impact of foreign cultures. Critics of government policy maintain that a culture that must rely on government intervention for its survival does not deserve governmental support.

Test Yourself

A. *Identification*:   Explain the meaning and/or significance of the following in your own words.

identity   culture
Canadian content regulations   dominant culture

B. *True And False*:   Indicate with the letter T or the letter F whether you think the following statements are accurate or inaccurate. If any part of the statement is false or inaccurate, use the letter F.

1. English-speaking Canadians prefer to watch American television.
2. English-language Canadian television seldom depicts Canadian minority groups.
3. English-language Canadian television consistently depicts some minority group members in a negative way.
4. The majority of news announcers are white males.
5. A nation's identity is transmitted by its media of mass communication.
6. English-speaking Canadians watch American news more than Canadian news.
7. Canadian content regulations have significantly lessened the influence of American ideas in Canada.
8. Some people believe that Canadian content restrictions prevent valuable cross-cultural contact.

C. *Multiple Choice*:   For each question indicate which response you think best answers the question.

1. English-speaking Canadians spend most of their viewing time watching:

    a. sporting events.

    b. variety and quiz programs.

    c. news and public affairs programs.

    d. dramatic programs.

2. If viewers see members of their culture consistently depicted in a negative way on television:

    a. they will learn to resent the majority culture.

    b. they will not learn about their own culture.

    c. they may come to believe the negative image shown on television.

    d. they will probably stop watching the programs that depict their group in a negative way.

3. English-language Canadian television:

    a. stereotypes the members of many ethnic groups.

    b. represents ethnic groups in proportion to their numbers in Canadian society.

    c. is inconsistent in its depiction of ethnic groups in Canada.

    d. over-represents white males of Anglo descent.

4. Non-white minorities depicted in television advertising:

    a. promote products exclusively for members of their own group.

    b. are often stereotyped as hungry, needy people.

    c. are depicted as happy, confident people.

    d. are often depicted as intolerant members of other ethnic groups.

5. Which group is most subject to stereotyping and under-representation on English-language Canadian television?

    a. women

    b. blacks

    c. native Canadians

    d. Asians

D. *Activities For Further Investigation*

1. Canadian content regulations have been the subject of debate since their passage in 1967. Investigate the history of Canadian content regulations. Why were they enacted? To what extent have the regulations achieved the objectives for which they were developed? Discuss the reactions of various groups to these regulations, including Canadian and foreign artists, producers, politicians and the public. Conclude by stating your position about Canadian content regulations. Do you favour the elimination, reduction or extension of these regulations?

2. There is considerable debate among observers of the Canadian scene about the existence of a uniquely Canadian identity. After reading about the subject, write an essay in which you address the problem of Canadian identity. If you believe that one exists, identify the characteristics of the Canadian identity and the factors you believe have helped shape that identity. If you conclude that there is no Canadian identity, attempt to explain why Canada, unlike most other nations, does not have a national identity.

3. Discuss the following in class. What responsibility do you think television has to accurately portray Canadian life? How well does English-language television fulfil this role? What benefits are gained for Canadians when television performs well in this respect? What are the dangers for Canadians if television fails in this respect?

4. The Broadcasting Act prohibits "any abusive comment or abusive pictorial representation of any race, religion, or creed." Discuss how well you think English-language Canadian television meets this regulation. Do you think the regulation is or is not necessary?

Television And Its Critics

As we have seen throughout this book, television today occupies a central place in Canadian society. People rely heavily on it for their entertainment and for information. Given the importance people attach to television, it is not surprising that it has been frequently criticized.

The American radio comedian Fred Allen once said, "They call television a medium because almost none of it is well done." Bertrand Russell, an English philosopher, called television "chewing gum for the eyes." Television has been criticized in books and magazines as well as in movies such as *Network* and *Being There*.

The novel, and movie, *Being There* is a story about a man whose main source of knowledge about the world is television. The man, named Chance, has lived his entire life within the walls of an estate. Lacking formal education and contact with people outside of the estate, Chance can neither read nor write. He responds to his world entirely on the basis of what he has seen on television.

When the owner of the estate dies, Chance can no longer remain within the estate's walls. Fearful that Chance will claim that he should share in the settlement of the owner's property, a lawyer asks Chance to sign a contract giving up any claim:

> Chance picked up the paper. He held it in both hands and stared at it. He tried to calculate the time needed to read a page. On TV the time it took people to read legal papers varied. Chance knew that he should not reveal that he could not read or write. On TV programs people who did not know how to read or write were often mocked and ridiculed. He assumed a look of concentration .... "I can't sign it," he said, returning the sheet to the lawyer. "I just can't."

Television's impact on children has long been the subject of great concern and study.

Taking his cues from what he has seen on television, Chance makes his way in the world. Through a series of accidents, he comes to be associated with a very wealthy businessman. People take the simple things Chance has learned to say from watching television as important comments about the world.

Eventually Chance becomes a celebrity. He appears on a talk-show and becomes friendly with the President of the United States. When the Vice-President of the United States decides not to seek re-election, Chance is considered as a candidate.

Being There is as much a satire of people's willingness to accept shallowness in others as it is a satire of the shallowness of television. Nevertheless, in an entertaining way, *Being There* raises some questions about television's influence on people.

From the first television broadcasts until today, people have expressed concern about the quality of television and its effect on viewers. Children have often been the focal point for much of the concern. Some people argue that because children lack experience and education they are especially vulnerable to what is presented on television.

Some of the concerns expressed about children and television are based on two observations. The first is that children's preference for television content shifts from child-oriented programs to adult-oriented programs at an early age. The second is that after they have been exposed to adult-oriented programs, most children do not continue to watch children's programs.

People are worried about exposing young children to adult-oriented programs because they think adult programs are often violent, stereotypic and unrealistic.

Television And Violence

Critics have been particularly concerned about violence on television. They suggest that television programs give viewers two

Physical pain — details of physical injury or death — is shown to be a consequence of violence in only one out of every four violent acts. In television drama violence does not hurt too much, nor are its consequences very bloody or messy, even though it may lead to injury or death.

Independent analysis of dramatic television programs for United States National Commission on the Causes and Prevention of Violence

inaccurate impressions about violence. First, they give the impression that there is more violence in the world than there really is. Second, they give the impression that violence is an acceptable solution to the problems that people face. Television programs also present violence in a misleading, unrealistic way. People involved in fistfights, beatings and shootings of the sort shown on television dramas would be much more seriously hurt and would suffer for much longer periods of time than do the heroes and heroines, and even the villains, on television programs. Analysts suggest that the constant repetition of violent images reinforces incorrect impressions about people and the world.

A frequent and regular viewer of television today might gain the impression that it is necessary and acceptable to use force to preserve community values. And, although this impression may be accurate to a limited extent when applied to many Canadian and American communities, viewers who often watch television will probably overestimate the number of times force will actually be needed.

Research seems to indicate that adolescents who frequently watch television express more fear than those who seldom watch. Viewers reflect their fearfulness in their tendency to overestimate the number of people involved with violence and the number of times the police use violence. The fact that violence is a frequent and constant feature of television seems to support the association of fearfulness with the presence of violence on television.

The possible effect on the viewer of television violence has been an important issue since the moment television was introduced. Yet despite this early concern, some of the many changes in television over the years relate directly to television's increasing use of violence to create and maintain viewer involvement.

During the early days of television, live programming was commonplace. Viewer involvement in dramatic programming was achieved by creating psychological tension. Psychological tension

---

■ Investigation 10.1: *To Find Out Whether The Amount Of Television People Watch Influences The Amount Of Violence They Think Takes Place In Canadian Society*

Method:

1. Arrange to sample the opinions of about 100 people, using a questionnaire similar to Appendix X.

2. Arrange your data from the opinion survey according to the amount of viewing time reported by each person questioned. A sample tabulation sheet entitled "Amount of Television Viewing and the Perception of Violence in Canadian Society" is included in Appendix XI. You will need to consult the most recent Canadian almanac to obtain actual crime statistics for comparison.

3. Write a general statement describing the apparent relationship between the amount of television viewing people do and the amount of violence they think occurs in Canada.

4. In a short essay, speculate about possible connections between a person's viewing habits and the amount of violence he or she feels exists in Canadian society.

Skills Developed: **3.2; 3.3; 3.5; 4.2; 4.3; 4.4**

---

is tension created in the mind of the viewer by getting the viewer to become concerned about a problem being faced by the main character.

In other words, in live television, suspense was created by presenting the viewer with characters who faced problems which seemed difficult to overcome. As film and tape became the main methods of television production, replacing live broadcasts, writers and directors were able to use additional techniques to create tension. Film and tape allowed them to use rapid scene changes and action sequences to create and increase tension.

As television developed, more and more of the action sequences involved violent or aggressive behaviour. Fights, car chases, scenes of battle and similar material became increasingly common.

Assessing the impact of television violence is difficult. Many factors must be present in a situation to lead most people to respond in a violent or aggressive manner. There are, nevertheless, several reasonable assumptions that may be made about television's influence on behaviour.

People learn from the experiences they have. Television is a common and frequent experience for most Canadians. It is reasonable that, under certain conditions, a person's inclination toward aggressive or violent behaviour can be affected by television. If, for example, a person sees violence used on television over and over again as a way of controlling undesirable behaviour in others, the person may more readily accept its use in his or her own real community.

It is also reasonable to assume that a person's estimation of the outcome of violent or aggressive behaviour can be influenced by what that person sees on television. For example, if a viewer constantly sees someone's position improve because that person used violence or behaved aggressively, the viewer might be persuaded to adopt a similar strategy to improve his or her own position.

The tension and excitement created by some television programs might cause someone to respond violently to a situation, even though that is not the person's normal reaction. In other words, after seeing a particularly violent program and becoming excited by it, a person who is faced with a problem might use violence to solve the problem, even though that is not the person's typical response to problems.

Critics charge that television suggests that violence is an acceptable method of dealing with problems. Scene from CBC's *Seeing Things*, starring Louis Del Grande as Louie Ciccone.

■ **Investigation 10.2:** | *To Determine The Underlying Assumptions About The Use Of Violence On Television*

Method:

1. Select a number of television programs in which violence plays a prominent part.

2. Systematically observe the television programs, noting when, where, how and why violence has been used. Use a "Conflict Observation Record" similar to Appendix XII to make a systematic record of your observations.

3. Prepare a report summarizing your findings. Your report should include a section in which you discuss what television seems to tell viewers about when it is acceptable and when it is not acceptable to use violence.

4. In your report you may wish to compare your observations about television violence with the same kind of systematic observations about conflicts that occur around you each day. For example, you might observe the conflicts which typically occur on a playground.

Skills Developed: | **2.6; 3.3; 3.4; 4.1; 4.3**

Using violence to maintain viewer interest is a feature of filmed or videotaped television production. During the early years of television when television dramas were presented as live performances, violence was not often used to maintain viewer interest. Dramatic programs maintained high viewer involvement by using other techniques. In other words, the present levels of television violence are not necessary to achieve viewer interest.

There are, nevertheless, times when violence is a central element in a plot and not simply a device to maintain the viewer's interest. Under such circumstances, the presentation of violence is necessary because it fits the larger context.

In May 1976 the Ontario government, in response to growing demands from a concerned public, established a Royal Commission on Violence in the Communications Industry. Here the members of the Commission, Judy LaMarsh, Scott Young *(left)* and Judge Lucien Beauline, consider the results of their hearings.

On the whole, the rich people on prime time are not the beautiful people. While they may be lovely superficially, they will be scheming, unhappy people who would just as soon commit murder as buy an original Renoir.

BEN STEIN, *The View from Sunset Boulevard*

It is important to see televised violence in the context of all the programming that is presented on television. In other words, although present levels of televised violence are not necessary, these violent actions take place within programs which show other values as well.

Most television violence takes place within programs that have similar characteristics. In the vast majority of dramatic programs, for example, good wins out over evil. In most television productions, fair treatment is also emphasized. Although in early television drama, fair treatment was less often an issue of importance, today the practice of safeguarding the rights of people accused of crimes is a regular feature of television productions about or involving the police. It is true, however, that the police are sometimes presented as being reluctant to safeguard these rights.

Television Versus "Real Life"

The amount of violence on television programming is not the only reason people criticize television. Critics also accuse television of presenting individuals and situations unrealistically and stereotypically. In other words, television presents people as "types" rather than as complicated human beings, and situations as much simpler than they are in real life.

The presentation of women on television has been particularly criticized. Women have generally been shown in a much less favourable and a more stereotyped way than other groups. Many critics argue that television has reinforced sexism in its treatment of women.

The women presented on television are often presented as being much less competent than their real-life counterparts. Even on the few dramatic programs featuring women in important positions, the women presented are more likely to need the help

---

■ Investigation 10.3:

To Determine Whether Television Presents Men And Women In A Stereotypic Fashion

Method:

1.   Select a dramatic program.

2.   Systematically observe the attributes or traits portrayed by the men and women in that program. Use a characterization check list similar to Appendix V to record your observations.

3.   Prepare your data for presentation to the class. Based on your findings include in your report your answer to the following question: *Are some characteristics attributed to women which are not attributed to men and vice versa?*

Skills Developed: **1.22; 1.23; 3.1; 4.2; 4.3**

---

of men to complete a task than the other way around. Commercials have often reinforced the stereotype of women as interested only in household cleansers, grocery shopping, and preparing meals. Television drama and advertisements have both tended to feature young, attractive women and to ignore older women.

Men, too, have been treated as stereotypes. They are interested in sports, not symphonies. They are strong and tough, not gentle and sensitive. In short, according to many analysts television has generally presented women and men as one-dimensional people. It has not reflected the human being's vast variety and complexity.

In its presentation of family situations, too, television drama is accused of being unrealistic and stereotypic. Taken as a group, the families on television have fewer problems than real-life families. The problems television families have are often less severe and are usually more easily overcome than those of real families.

Occupations are also presented unrealistically and stereotypically. For example, when the occupations of people on television can be determined, it is more likely that the occupation will be in the managerial or professional categories than in the category of workers who have industrial jobs.

On television, people seem to take on the characteristics which are associated with their work. For example, people presented as working in law enforcement are typically shown as being less sympathetic toward others than are the people presented as working in medicine-related jobs.

■ **Investigation 10.4:**	*To Determine How The Television Family Influences The Values And Attitudes Of Its Members*
Method:	1. Select one or more television programs that focus on a family group.
	3. Systematically observe the programs to determine the values and attitudes of the family members.
	3. In a short essay, describe the values and attitudes which all members of the family share, the values and attitudes which are shared only by the men or only by the women in the family, and the values and attitudes which are shared only by the parents or only by the children.
	4. Your essay should attempt to answer the following questions:
	a. Do the attitudes and values of family members change? What prompts changes in family attitudes and values?
	b. How do the patterns observed among the members of television families compare with the patterns in your own family?
Skills Developed:	**1.22; 1.23; 2.6; 3.2; 3.3; 3.4; 4.1**

■ Investigation 10.5: *To Identify How Language Is Used On Television*

Method:

1.   Scripts of television programs are often available from the producer. Write to a producer of one program in each programming category to obtain a sample script for classroom use. Be certain to indicate why you are requesting the script and that its use will be confined to the classroom.

2.   While you are waiting for the scripts to arrive, arrange to record conversations as they normally occur in a variety of settings. For example, with people's consent, record conversations at the dinner table, between sales clerks and customers in a store, among friends eating in a fast food restaurant.

3.   From your recordings, select two conversations of about two minutes in length. Type the recordings as if they were part of a script.

4.   When you have obtained a television script, examine it closely. Notice the length of the sentences, the choice of words and the way the sentences are constructed.

5.   Compare the scripts from the television programs with the typescripts of the conversations you recorded. Carefully note any similarities and differences you observe.

6.   Prepare an essay in which you present the result of your study. Your essay should address the similarities and differences that can be observed between the way people talk on television and the way they talk in "real-life" situations.

7.   Exchange essays with other class members.

Skills Developed: 1.15; 1.22; 1.23; 1.26; 1.27; 3.1; 3.3; 4.1; 4.2; 4.3; 4.4; 4.5

Television presents people as types and simplifies situations for the purpose of telling the viewer a story. In other words, television purposely distorts things in the same way that it uses devices such as violence, rapidly paced cuts, and background music for dramatic effect.

Novels and short stories use similar techniques in the process of storytelling. The dialogue people read in a novel or hear spoken on television, for example, is more compressed and often more straightforward than the conversations people have in real life.

■ **Investigation 10.6:** *To Recognize The Limitations Of The Way Television Presents Solutions To Life's Problems*

Method: **In life, most people choose their response to a situation from a number of alternatives. Television typically presents a single response to a situation without showing the alternatives that might have been considered by the character.**

1. Select one of your favourite dramatic television programs as the focus for this exercise.
2. Describe a problem facing the central character in the story. Describe the alternatives the character considered in arriving at the solution he or she chose.
3. Outline as many alternative solutions as *you* can think of for the problem facing the main character.
4. Rewrite the script showing a different solution to the problems and any other related changes.
5. In a brief essay, address the question: *What does television tell viewers about the complexity of human problems?*

Skills Developed: **1.11; 1.12; 1.13; 1.21; 1.22; 3.3**

CTV's *Canada AM*, Canada's only live, national early morning news and information program, takes Canadians to where the news is happening, with on-location reports and interviews with world newsmakers, politicians and celebrities. *From left to right*, the *Canada AM* team: Sandie Rinaldo, Norm Perry, Wally Macht, and Pamela Wallin.

Radio, once a form of group listening that emptied churches, has reverted to private and individual uses since [the advent of] TV.

Coping With the Mass Media

The video cassette revolution is hardly an adequate description for a technological upheaval that will likely do to television what television did to radio.

GENE YOUNGBLOOD

Most everyday conversation contains many more "ums" and "ahs" than the conversations people read in novels or hear on television.

People in novels and on television get to the point of their conversation faster than real people do. If dialogue was not compressed, novels and television programs would go on and on. People would become bored and lose interest.

Concern about the way television distorts people and situations and presents such things as violence needs to be seen in perspective. If viewers were like Chance in *Being There*, there would be reason for concern. Chance responds to the world entirely in the ways he has seen people on television respond. Chance did not have other models of how to behave. He did not have a family to guide him and he did not go to school. He could not read or write. He grew up with television and had no other sources of information about the world.

Very few television viewers are like Chance. Although they may have grown up with television, they have other models of appropriate behaviour and many other sources of information about the world.

Looking Ahead

Television is a rapidly changing medium. During the preparation of this book alone several important changes occurred. During that period women began to receive more important roles in news programs. Today there are women anchoring or co-anchoring the national news desk, giving weather reports, reporting sports news, and hosting or co-hosting such news programs as CBC's *The Journal* and CTV's *Canada AM*. Television stations began to broadcast more multicultural programming, for the first time giving some of Canada's cultural minorities a meaningful

The Sony Watchman TV with a 5-cm screen is a pocket-size black and white television.

role in television drama and news. Several pay television stations were licensed. And, no sooner had that change been reflected in the text than one of the stations went out of business. As the book was first taking shape, one manufacturer of television equipment announced the development of a television set which was the size of a pocket calculator. Several months later, the set was selling for $400.00. Today, the same set is advertised at less than $150.00.

While the impact of television on Canadian society has been significant, it is almost certain that further changes will occur. These changes may produce consequences for Canada and Canadians which are even more far-reaching than those described in this book.

In studying *Television and Society* you will have developed an understanding of how the systems in society — technological, political, economic, social, and intellectual — are interconnected. You will have developed the skills to investigate and analyze how change in one of the systems affects changes in the other systems. In particular you will have assessed how the technological changes brought about by the development of television have affected changes in all areas of Canadian life. You will be able to consider intelligently the role television has played and is playing in your own life. And you will be able to suggest the role you think television should play and how it can be improved.

As a member of this society, you are obliged to look ahead toward the changes which may be produced by developments such as television. You need to evaluate the impact that such changes will have on the society in which you live. By taking part in public debate about issues related to the control of technology, you will be actively helping to shape the world in which you will live your life.

Test Yourself

A. *True And False*: Indicate with the letter T or the letter F whether you think the following statements are accurate or inaccurate. If any part of the statement is false or inaccurate, use the letter F.

1. Script writers inject violence into stories because they believe that violence is an acceptable means with which to solve problems.

2. Television may lead some viewers to accept violence as a means of solving problems.

3. Television exaggerates the occurrence of violence in everyday life.

4. Violence has been a major ingredient in television dramas since the early days of television.

5. There is never justification for the use of violence in television programs.

6. Dialogue on television is generally more straightforward and concise than everyday conversation.

7. It would be impossible to produce interesting dramatic programs if violence were not permitted on television.

B. *Activities For Further Investigation:*

1. In an essay, explain what you think of when you hear or read the term "made-for-TV movie." Has your view of "made-for-TV movies" changed since such movies first appeared? Explain your answer.

2. You may have seen television programs or movies based on novels you have read. Compare your reaction to the book with your reaction to the film production. What changes were made to adapt the book to a visual medium?

3. Read *Being There* by Jerzy Kosinski and write an essay summarizing the book's comments about the impact of television on society.

4. Discuss the following statement: "Television reflects rather than shapes society's values."

5. What factors other than television violence may influence a person to exhibit violent behaviour? Do you think violence should be banned from or extremely limited on television?

6. The advent of pay television in Canada saw the nation-wide telecast of adult programming (Playboy Channel) for Canadian viewers. While the programming was not sexually explicit and was played only late at night, it raised an outcry across Canada. In early 1983, First Choice dropped its Playboy programming, although it denied that its decision was prompted by public pressure. Research the debate about adult programming on pay television. For your discussion some of you should examine the provisions of the Canadian Criminal Code concerning pornography.

7. Many of you will one day be parents and will have to establish a policy about the role of television in your home. Write a short essay describing the guidelines, if any, you would establish for your children. Explain the reasons for establishing or not establishing guidelines.

Appendices

APPENDIX I *Skills Developed by Doing the Investigations*

1.0 Comprehension Skills

1.1 Literal Comprehension
1.11 Identify the main idea and supporting details in a visual form.
1.12 Identify the sequence of events in a visual form.
1.13 Identify the characters, setting and events presented in a narrative context.
1.14 Identify the stated purpose of a communication.
1.15 Compare ideas, characters, themes, events and processes.
1.16 Identify various narrative forms.

1.2 Inferential Comprehension
1.21 Predict outcomes from the events which preceded.
1.22 Draw conclusions from information presented.
1.23 Generalize from a variety of instances.
1.24 Identify the implied purpose of the communication.
1.25 Identify cause and effect relationships.
1.26 Compare ideas, events, characters, themes and purposes.
1.27 Identify the use of figurative language.

2.0 Evaluative Skills

2.1 Distinguish between factual and evaluative claims.
2.2 Determine the accuracy of the information presented.

2.3 Identify the persuasive techniques used in communication.
2.4 Distinguish between relevant and irrelevant information.
2.5 Identify bias in communication.
2.6 Compare own values with those of others.
2.7 Construct and test hypotheses.

3.0 Composing Skills

3.1 Present information in a variety of written forms, including essays, tables, graphs, charts, and diagrams.
3.2 Write descriptive, expository, narrative and argumentative paragraphs.
3.3 Write multi-paragraph compositions that are coherent and logical.
3.4 Present and defend a point of view.
3.5 Construct a reasoned argument presenting several sides of an issue.

4.0 Research and Study Skills

4.1 Locate and use information from primary and secondary sources.
4.2 Construct and use a variety of means for collecting data systematically.
4.3 Record data accurately.
4.4 Classify and organize pertinent information in a meaningful way.
4.5 Organize and combine information from a variety of sources for presentation.
4.6 Interpret tables, charts and graphs.

Reproduced from Charles S. Ungerleider and Ernest Krieger, *Television and Society: An Investigative Approach*, with permission of Irwin Publishing Inc., Toronto, Canada.

APPENDIX II   *Public Attitudes Toward Pay Television*

1. Have you ever subscribed to pay television?

[   ]   Yes, I currently subscribe to pay television.*

[   ]   Yes, I subscribed in the past, but not now.*

[   ]   No, I have never subscribed to pay television.*

*If you answered "yes" to the question above, please answer questions 1.1 to question 2 and question 4. If you answered "no," please skip to questions 3 and 4.

1.1 What was your main reason for subscribing to pay television?

[   ]   I can gain access to content that is not available on other channels.

[   ]   I want(ed) commercial-free programming.

[   ]   The quality of programming on pay television is superior to the programming on commercial/public television.

[   ]   I was persuaded to subscribe to pay television by promotional material.

[   ]   Pay television is available as part of my housing arrangements (i.e., included in rental fee).

[   ]   The low cost of the pay television service encouraged me to subscribe.

1.2 What programs on pay television do you most frequently watch?

[   ]   movies

[   ]   sports

[   ]   cultural programming (plays, music, theatre)

[   ]   adult programming

[   ]   other (please specify) _____

1.3 How well has pay television met your expectations?

[   ]   satisfies my expectations very well*

[   ]   satisfies my expectations*

[   ]   does not satisfy my expectations*

*If you answered "does not satisfy" to the question above, please answer question 1.4. If you answered "satisfies," please skip to question 2.

1.4 If you have not been satisfied by pay television, what factor has contributed most to your dissatisfaction?

[   ]   poor selection of programs

[   ]   poor scheduling of programs

[   ]   lack of varied programming

[   ]   too much Canadian content

[   ]   too little Canadian content

[   ]   too much adult programming

[   ]   other (please specify) _____

2. Since acquiring pay television service, I

[   ]   watch more television.

[   ]   watch less television.

[   ]   do not watch as much commercial/public television as I used to.

[   ]   have increased my appreciation for commercial/public television.

Reproduced from Charles S. Ungerleider and Ernest Krieger, *Television and Society: An Investigative Approach*, with permission of Irwin Publishing Inc., Toronto, Canada.

3. If you answered "no" to question 1, please indicate your reason for not subscribing to pay television.

I do not subscribe to pay television because:

[   ]   it isn't available in my community.

[   ]   it is too expensive.

[   ]   it does not provide the programming I most enjoy.

[   ]   other (please specify) _____

4. Approximately how many hours per week do you watch television?

[   ]   less than ten hours per week

[   ]   ten to nineteen hours per week

[   ]   twenty to twenty-nine hours per week

[   ]   thirty to thirty-nine hours per week

[   ]   forty or more hours per week

APPENDIX III *Reaction Ballot*

DIRECTIONS: Circle the number that comes closest to expressing your reaction to what you have just seen.

SERIOUS   7 : 6 : 5 : 4 : 3 : 2 : 1   FUNNY

If you thought that what you saw was very serious, you would circle the number closest to the word serious (#7). If you thought that what you saw was very funny, you would circle the number closest to the word funny (#1). If you thought that what you saw was between serious and funny, you would circle number 4.

HAPPY	7 : 6 : 5 : 4 : 3 : 2 : 1	SAD
FRIENDLY	7 : 6 : 5 : 4 : 3 : 2 : 1	UNFRIENDLY
BORING	1 : 2 : 3 : 4 : 5 : 6 : 7	INTERESTING
DISHONEST	1 : 2 : 3 : 4 : 5 : 6 : 7	HONEST
RELIABLE	7 : 6 : 5 : 4 : 3 : 2 : 1	UNRELIABLE
FAIR	7 : 6 : 5 : 4 : 3 : 2 : 1	UNFAIR
LARGE	7 : 6 : 5 : 4 : 3 : 2 : 1	SMALL
CONFUSING	1 : 2 : 3 : 4 : 5 : 6 : 7	CLEAR
PLEASANT	7 : 6 : 5 : 4 : 3 : 2 : 1	UNPLEASANT
WEAK	1 : 2 : 3 : 4 : 5 : 6 : 7	STRONG

APPENDIX IV *Tabulation Sheet for Reaction Ballot Example*

	Category Value	Number of times category was picked	Category Value × Number of times category was picked
Sad	1	× 1	= 1
	2	× 4	= 8
	3	× 10	= 30
	4	× 8	= 32
	5	× 9	= 45
	6	× 5	= 30
Happy	7	× 3	= 21
		40	167

STEP 1. Count the number of times each category value was picked and record it opposite the category value.

STEP 2. Multiply the category value times the number of times the category value was selected.

STEP 3. Add the number of times all the categories were picked. Call this the "N" for the number of picks (N = 40).

STEP 4. Add the values determined by multiplying category values times the number of times each was selected. Call this the "total" (total = 167).

STEP 5. Divide the total (167) by the N (40). The result is the average response for the item (167/40 = 4.175).

In the example, the average response is just slightly to the "happy" side of position "4" between sad and happy on the scale presented in Appendix III.

	Category Value	Number of times category was picked	Category Value × Number of times category was picked
Sad	1	×	=
	2	×	=
	3	×	=
	4	×	=
	5	×	=
	6	×	=
Happy	7	×	=

APPENDIX V *Characterization Check List*

Program _____   Date _____

Station _____   Time _____

Observer _____

	Character	*Character*	*Character*	*Character*
Name	_____	_____	_____	_____
	[ ] Female	[ ] Female	[ ] Female	[ ] Female
	[ ] Male	[ ] Male	[ ] Male	[ ] Male
Cultural Group:	_____	_____	_____	_____

Trait or Attribute:

Trait				
Happy	[ ]	[ ]	[ ]	[ ]
Sad	[ ]	[ ]	[ ]	[ ]
Friendly	[ ]	[ ]	[ ]	[ ]
Unfriendly	[ ]	[ ]	[ ]	[ ]
Boring	[ ]	[ ]	[ ]	[ ]
Interesting	[ ]	[ ]	[ ]	[ ]
Dishonest	[ ]	[ ]	[ ]	[ ]
Honest	[ ]	[ ]	[ ]	[ ]
Reliable	[ ]	[ ]	[ ]	[ ]
Unreliable	[ ]	[ ]	[ ]	[ ]
Fair	[ ]	[ ]	[ ]	[ ]
Unfair	[ ]	[ ]	[ ]	[ ]
Large	[ ]	[ ]	[ ]	[ ]
Small	[ ]	[ ]	[ ]	[ ]
Confusing	[ ]	[ ]	[ ]	[ ]
Unconfusing	[ ]	[ ]	[ ]	[ ]
Pleasant	[ ]	[ ]	[ ]	[ ]
Unpleasant	[ ]	[ ]	[ ]	[ ]
Weak	[ ]	[ ]	[ ]	[ ]
Strong	[ ]	[ ]	[ ]	[ ]
Attractive	[ ]	[ ]	[ ]	[ ]
Unattractive	[ ]	[ ]	[ ]	[ ]
Competent	[ ]	[ ]	[ ]	[ ]
Incompetent	[ ]	[ ]	[ ]	[ ]
Lazy	[ ]	[ ]	[ ]	[ ]
Energetic	[ ]	[ ]	[ ]	[ ]

APPENDIX VI *Media Believability*

1. Please rank the following SOURCES OF NEWS INFORMATION according to the amount of time you devote to them. Rank the most used medium as number "1", the next most used medium as number "2", and so on.

   RANK   MEDIUM

   _____ Magazines

   _____ Newspapers

   _____ Radio

   _____ Television

2. Please rank the following SOURCES OF ADVERTISING INFORMATION according to the amount of use you make of them. Rank the most used medium as number "1", the next most used medium as number "2", and so on.

   RANK   MEDIUM

   _____ Magazines

   _____ Newspapers

   _____ Radio

   _____ Television

3. Please rank the following SOURCES OF NEWS INFORMATION according to how accurately you think they present information. Rank the medium which is most accurate as number "1", the second most accurate source as number "2", and so on.

   RANK   MEDIUM

   _____ Magazines

   _____ Newspapers

   _____ Radio

   _____ Television

4. Please rank the following SOURCES OF ADVERTISING INFORMATION according to how accurately you think they present information. Rank the medium which is most accurate as number "1", the second most accurate source as number "2", and so on.

   RANK   MEDIUM

   _____ Magazines

   _____ Newspapers

   _____ Radio

   _____ Television

5. It would be helpful to my study to know the following information:

Sex: [ ] Female   [ ] Male

Age: [ ] 10-19 years of age
        [ ] 20-29 years of age
        [ ] 30-39 years of age
        [ ] 40-49 years of age
        [ ] 50-59 years of age
        [ ] 60-69 years of age
        [ ] 70 years or older

Education: Please check the highest level of schooling you have had.

        [ ] did not complete elementary school
        [ ] completed elementary school
        [ ] did not complete high school
        [ ] completed high school
        [ ] enrolled in a technical program after high school
        [ ] completed a technical program after high school
        [ ] enrolled in a university program
        [ ] completed a university program

Occupation:
        What is your usual job or occupation? _____

Television Viewing: Check the category indicating the amount of television viewing you do in an average week.

        [ ] 0-10 hours per week
        [ ] 11-20 hours per week
        [ ] 21-30 hours per week
        [ ] 31-40 hours per week
        [ ] 41 or more hours per week

APPENDIX VII *News Analysis Guide Sheet*

Date _____   Station _____

Time _____   (   ) National or (   ) Local

Item	Length of Item min:sec	Region of Focus						Topic of Focus							Perform-ers		Production Features				
		International	National	Provincial	Regional	Local	Feature	Political	Economic	Social	Intellectual	Technological	Sports	Weather	Knowns	Unknowns	Film/tape	Slide/graphic	Audio clip	News reader	News analyst

APPENDIX VIII *Political Advertising on Television*

Date	Time	Length of Advertisement (in seconds)	Station	Candidate/ Party	Issue	Image
					[ ]	[ ]
					[ ]	[ ]
					[ ]	[ ]
					[ ]	[ ]
					[ ]	[ ]
					[ ]	[ ]
					[ ]	[ ]
					[ ]	[ ]
					[ ]	[ ]
					[ ]	[ ]
					[ ]	[ ]
					[ ]	[ ]

APPENDIX IX   *A Guide for Analyzing Advertising on Television*

Name of product advertised ___ _____

Station on which advertised _____

Date _____   Time _____   Observer _____

The product presentation was made by a:
[ ] man [ ] woman

The age of the person making the presentation was:
[ ] 0-10 years of age
[ ] 11-20 years of age
[ ] 21-30 years of age
[ ] 31-40 years of age
[ ] 41-50 years of age
[ ] 51-60 years of age
[ ] 61 years of age or older
[ ] could not determine age

The person who made the presentation was depicted as behaving:
[ ] passively
[ ] actively
[ ] aggressively
[ ] cannot determine

The product was [ ] or was not [ ] associated with appeal to members of the opposite sex.

The use of the product was associated with increased:
[ ] masculinity
[ ] femininity
[ ] could not determine

The person depicted in the advertisement was represented as working as a _____ .

The following techniques were used in the advertisement:
[ ] implied promise
[ ] implied superiority
[ ] image advertising
[ ] testimonial
[ ] bandwagon
[ ] plain folks

Write a brief statement evaluating the usefulness of the product in relation to the claims made about it.

Reproduced from Charles S. Ungerleider and Ernest Krieger, *Television and Society: An Investigative Approach*, with permission of Irwin Publishing Inc., Toronto, Canada.

APPENDIX X   *A Survey of Opinion About Crime and Television Viewing in Canada*

Listed below are some questions about crime and television viewing in Canada. You can help by answering the questions to the best of your ability. Please do not record your name anywhere on this survey. Your answers will be confidential.

1. Which of the following comes closest to the annual murder rate for every 100 000 Canadians?
[   ] a. approximately 5 murders per 100 000 Canadians
[   ] b. approximately 10 murders per 100 000 Canadians
[   ] c. approximately 50 murders per 100 000 Canadians
[   ] d. approximately 100 murders per 100 000 Canadians

2. Which of the following comes closest to the annual robbery rate for every 100 000 Canadians?
[   ] a. approximately 25 robberies per 100 000 Canadians
[   ] b. approximately 50 robberies per 100 000 Canadians
[   ] c. approximately 100 robberies per 100 000 Canadians
[   ] d. approximately 250 robberies per 100 000 Canadians

3. Which of the following comes closest to the annual rate for drug offences for every 100 000 Canadians?
[   ] a. approximately 50 drug offences per 100 000 Canadians
[   ] b. approximately 100 drug offences per 100 000 Canadians
[   ] c. approximately 250 drug offences per 100 000 Canadians
[   ] d. approximately 500 drug offences per 100 000 Canadians

4. Approximately how many hours per week do you spend watching television?
[   ] a. approximately 9 hours or less per week
[   ] b. approximately 10 to 19 hours per week
[   ] c. approximately 20 to 29 hours per week
[   ] d. approximately 30 to 39 hours per week
[   ] e. approximately 40 or more hours per week

APPENDIX XI *Amount of Television Viewing and the Perception of Violence in Canadian Society*

	Amount of Television Viewing per Week				
	0-9 Hours	10-19 Hours	20-29 Hours	30-39 Hours	40 or More
Murder Rate Estimates					
Below Actual					
Accurate					
Above Actual					
Robbery Rate Estimates					
Below Actual					
Accurate					
Above Actual					
Drug Offence Estimates					
Below Actual					
Accurate					
Above Actual					

APPENDIX XII   *Conflict Observation Record*

Program _____   Date _____

Station _____   Time _____

Observer _____

| What Caused the Violence? | What Action Took Place? | How Did the Conflict End? |

Reproduced from Charles S. Ungerleider and Ernest Krieger, *Television and Society: An Investigative Approach*, with permission of Irwin Publishing Inc., Toronto, Canada.

Glossary

Account executive the person in an advertising agency who serves as the contact person between the advertising agency and the advertiser.

Account group a group in an advertising agency made up of an account executive, creative director, media director, writer, producer and art director, responsible for producing a television commercial for a client.

Address code a time code used to separate locations on a videotape for editing purposes; the address code indicates each frame by hour, minute, second and frame number.

Ad-lib dialogue or action which is completely spontaneous and unrehearsed.

Affiliates independently owned stations which contract to telecast network programs.

Animation combining individual shots, still drawings or photographs to create pictures which give the impression of movement.

Antagonist the character in a story who works against the hero or heroine; the villain.

Anthology drama a series of unrelated dramas.

Aperture the opening in the camera lens that determines how much light passes through.

Arc movement of a camera in a curving pattern.

Art director the person in an advertising agency who is responsible for planning how a commercial message can achieve the greatest visual impact.

Assignment editor the person in a newsroom responsible for assigning reporters and camera crews to cover news events.

Audible loud enough to be heard.

Audio the sound portion of a television program.

Audio engineer technical person responsible for operating the audio (sound) equipment.

Audio level the strength of the audio signal.

Audio mix the combination of a number of audio signals to produce the desired sound.

Audition a trial performance in which actors and actresses, musicians, and so forth demonstrate their skills or suitability for a part, job, etc.; those performers who most closely match the producer's or director's needs are hired.

Autocuing devices *see Teleprompter*

Background light lighting of the set or background; also called "set light."

Background music music used to create a certain mood.

Backlight light from behind a subject.

Backtime the amount of time remaining in a show.

Bandwagon technique an advertising technique involving an appeal to people's desire to conform.

Batten a metal pipe from which lights are hung.

Boom microphone a microphone suspended on a long mechanical arm.

Break to release a camera to move to another position or to obtain another shot.

Breakaway prop a specially designed prop which will break harmlessly on impact.

Broadcast time the total amount of time devoted to broadcasting.

Cable television the transmission of television signals over wire.

Cameo a lighting technique in which foreground subjects appear before a completely black background.

Canted angle a scene shown from other than a horizontal plane.

Capital costs the cost of land, buildings and machines.

Cast the members of a company of performers.

Casting director person responsible for selecting performers for a television production.

Celebrity a person who is well known to the general public.

Censorship the removal from a broadcast of material which might be considered offensive.

Channel a special band or frequency assigned to a radio or television station.

Character generator a device which electronically produces lettering and other graphics directly onto a television screen.

Chromakeying (keying) an electronic process in which photographic material is combined with the image of a performer.

Chronology a table of events in the order of occurrence.

Close-up a camera shot in which the subject is close to the camera.

Comedy *see Situation comedy*.

Comprehensiveness (in news) breadth and depth of reporting.

Continuity the logical and smooth transition between parts of a production.

Control room the area where the program's director and production personnel control the production of a program.

Copy editor the person who edits reporters' reports and writes the script for the newscast.

Costuming the outfitting of performers in attire suited to the television production.

Creative director the person in an advertising agency who is responsible for translating the advertiser's ideas into a set of words or images.

Credit an acknowledgement of the work done by people in the production of a program.

CRTC Canadian Radio-television Telecommunications Commission; the body that regulates all broadcasting in Canada.

Cue the signal to begin a program, action, dialogue or other production activity.

Cue card (idiot card) a large card containing the dialogue used by a performer. It is located next to the camera lens so that the performer may read it while appearing to look at the camera.

Cut an instant change from one shot to another.

Cutaway a shot which focuses on a view other than the main action.

Decibel a unit of measurement of sound.

Definition the degree of sharpness in a television picture.

Demographics refers to the population characteristics of an audience, including sex, age, education level and economic status.

Depth of field the distance between the closest and the farthest objects that are in focus.

Dialogue a conversation between two or more people.

Director the person in charge of the production and editing of a program.

Dissolve the gradual blending of one scene into another.

Documentary a production which attempts to show things as they actually happen without staging or rehearsing.

Drama a presentation intended for acting which involves conflict.

Dress rehearsal the final rehearsal of a production. Full costumes are worn.

Drop a large piece of canvas or other material used for scenery backing.

Editing the process of assembling the sound and picture material for presentation to the viewer; the deletion, addition or rearrangement of materials to create a desired effect.

Episodic drama a series of dramas organized around a set of characters who appear regularly in each show.

Establishing shot the opening shot or scene acquainting the viewer with the surroundings.

Extreme close-up a shot in which the subject fills the screen.

Extreme long-shot a shot which depicts a vast area from a great distance.

Fade the gradual appearance or disappearance of an image from the screen.

Film/tape editor the person who arranges the material in the desired order.

Flashback (flashforward) a look backward or forward in time.

Flat a piece of scenery used as a background.

Floodlight light source which produces an even light over a large area.

Floor plan a scale drawing of the studio, used in planning a production.

Focus an adjustment of a camera lens to produce clear sights or images.

Foundation make-up the make-up base on which other cosmetics are applied.

Frame one individual picture; to position correctly in the field of view.

Geosynchronous orbit a satellite orbit that allows the satellite to maintain its position in relation to the earth's surface.

Gopher an assistant who is asked to "go for" things.

Graphic materials charts, still pictures, and the like.

Hand cue a silent hand signal.

High-angle shot a camera shot looking down on the subject.

High-camera angle positioning of the camera above the subject's eye level.

Illusion something that deceives by creating a false impression.

Image advertisement an advertisement emphasizing the visual aspects of a person, product or service.

Implied promise technique an advertising technique which suggests that the user of a product will be more attractive to others because he or she uses the product.

Interview a conversation in which a person, not always a reporter, asks someone questions.

Issue advertisement an advertisement in which the message is given a more important place than the visual or image aspects.

Key light the main source of light on a subject or scene.

Keying *see Chromakeying.*

Lead story the first item in a newscast.

Licence legal authorization or permission to do something.

Lighting personnel people responsible for lighting the set for a television production.

Lineup editor the person who has the responsibility of ordering the items in a newscast.

Live broadcast as it happens.

Long shot a shot taken from a distance.

Low-camera angle when the camera is positioned below the subject's eye level.

Mark tape placed on the studio floor to indicate to performers or camera operators where they should be standing.

Master scene script the script which gives a complete account of all the action and dialogue.

Matinee a performance taking place in the afternoon.

Media director the person in an advertising agency who is responsible for planning where to place an advertisement in order to reach the largest audience with the greatest frequency.

Microcomputer a computer adapted to home or small business use.

Microwave network a chain of transmission and receiving devices.

Montage scenes that are connected by similar ideas and appear one after the other.

Narrow-angle lens *see Telephoto lens*

Night editor person responsible for overseeing a news operation at night.

Noise unwanted audio or video signals which interfere with normal program broadcasting.

Normal-angle lens a lens which produces the same perspective and view as our eyes produce.

Normal-camera angle the angle showing the world as a person normally sees it.

One shot a shot of one person or subject.

Operating costs day-to-day costs, excluding investment in buildings, land and machines.

Pan movement of the camera in a horizontal plane.

Pay television television programming available only to people who pay a subscription fee.

Perspective a view that includes things in the distance as well as things nearby.

Pickup tube the central part in the television camera which changes light into electrical messages.

Plain folks   an advertising technique based on the idea that people will purchase products they see being used by ordinary, everyday people like themselves.

Plot   the sequence of events which make up a story.

Point-of-view shot   *see Subjective camera angle.*

Post-production   the phase of production when all the segments on a film are assembled and edited.

Prime time   period of peak viewing, defined by CRTC as the period between 6 p.m. and midnight.

Producer   the production team member responsible for the entire production.

Product disclaimer   specific information included in advertisements to warn viewers about some characteristics of the product, for example, that batteries are not included.

Production budget   all of the costs for a television production.

Program concept   the idea on which a production is based.

Property (prop)   furniture and objects used by the performers.

Property department   the people responsible for the storage and provision of the props used in a television production.

Protagonist   the hero or heroine of a story; usually the main character.

Rating   a statistical estimate of a program's popularity by sampling people's viewing preferences. It is usually expressed as a percentage of the number of households watching a television program to all households possessing televisions.

Rebroadcast transmitter   a device which receives a signal, re-amplifies the signal and transmits the signal to another receiver.

Reception   the process of taking in/receiving a sound or picture signal.

Reflected light   light bounced back from the surface of an object.

Rehearsal   a practice in preparation for a performance.

Riser   a platform used to produce multiple levels on a studio set.

Script   the written text of a broadcast used in a television production.

Sequence   a series of scenes or shots complete in themselves; within a sequence, events are shown in a continuous manner as in real life.

Sequence outline   the first form a script takes; the program is translated into words describing the action in sequence.

Serial   a dramatic format in which a regular set of characters confront problems that continue from episode to episode.

Set designer   the artist responsible for designing the set for a television production.

Setting   the place where the events of a story occur.

Shooting script   a script including all the technical details for filming a production.

Shot   the portion of a scene photographed with one camera at one time.

Shot shopper   a slang term for program directors who permit their camera operators freedom in selecting shots.

Show reel the final edited film or videotape reel which is shown to the public.

Signal transmission the process of sending picture and sound signals from one location to another, usually by means of microwave or satellite.

Situation comedy (sit. com.) a light, amusing drama with a happy ending.

Sneak slow fade-in of sound on film or tape.

Sound effects artificially produced sounds such as thunder, crickets chirping or dishes breaking.

Sponsor an advertiser who pays for the entire production of a program in which only his or her goods or services are advertised.

Spotlight (spot) a light that produces an intense beam which strikes a small area.

Spotter a person at an event such as a football game who helps the producer, director, or announcer to identify participants and important action.

Standupper a slang term for a news item delivered by a reporter on location talking directly into the camera.

Statistics numerical facts or data which have been collected and arranged for study.

Storyboard a pictorial outline which shows a drawing of each shot in the script with both picture and sound directions.

Stretch a command given to a performer when the director wants the dialogue slowed down.

Strike to remove scenery and equipment from a set when it is no longer needed.

Subjective camera angle use of the camera to show how a scene looks through the eyes of a character in a performance.

Superimposition (sooper, super) two shots, one on top of the other, which are on the screen at the same time.

Sweetening the sound track adding applause or laughter to a program's sound track.

Synthetic demand the desire to have something that is not prompted by one's day-to-day needs.

Take a single attempt to film a segment of a television production.

Technical crew the people responsible for the maintenance and operation of the audio and visual equipment used in television production.

Telecast the transmission of a television program.

Telecommunications communications from one point to another.

Telecommunications carriers companies involved in the transmission of sound, pictures and data.

Telephoto lens a narrow-angle lens which makes distant objects appear closer to the viewer than they are.

Teleprompter (autocuing device) a device which projects script on a screen near the camera so that a performer may read the script while appearing to look at the camera.

Teletext the transmission of graphic (print and visual) messages.

Testimonial an advertisement in which a well-known personality or authoritative expert makes a claim of superiority for a product.

Theme the underlying idea that a story communicates.

Tilt   a vertical movement of a camera.

Tracking   movement of the camera to follow a moving subject.

Video   the picture part of a television signal.

Video cassette (disc or tape)   recording material capable of storing recorded images and sound which can be played back at some later time.

Video engineer   technical person responsible for operating the video (picture) equipment.

Viewing time   the total amount of time devoted to viewing.

Villain   a character in a drama who opposes the hero or heroine, the antagonist.

Voice over   a message or narrative spoken by someone who does not appear on the screen.

Wide-angle lens   a lens which shows a very broad view of a scene.

Wipe   a change of scene accomplished by moving a new picture onto the screen vertically, diagonally, or horizontally.

Wire services   companies which gather news and transmit it telegraphically to subscribers.

Writer   the person responsible for developing the script.

Zoom   a smooth, usually rapid, change from a close-up to a long shot or vice versa.

Index